THE

Eddie Bauer

GUIDE TO
BACKPACKING

THE *Eddie Bauer*
GUIDE TO
BACKPACKING

ARCHIE SATTERFIELD and EDDIE BAUER

ILLUSTRATIONS BY TED RAND

ADDISON-WESLEY PUBLISHING COMPANY
READING, MASSACHUSETTS•MENLO PARK, CALIFORNIA
LONDON•AMSTERDAM•DON MILLS, ONTARIO•SYDNEY

Library of Congress Cataloging in Publication Data

Satterfield, Archie.
The Eddie Bauer guide to backpacking.

Bibliography: p.
1. Backpacking—Equipment and supplies.
I. Bauer, Eddie. II. Title. III. Title: Guide to backpacking.
GV199.62.S27 1983 796.5'1 83-5998
ISBN 0-201-07797-3
        0-201-07796-5-H

Design by Val Paul Taylor

Set in 10-point Lubalin by Crane Typesetting Service, Inc., Barnstable, MA

Production supervised by B&W Hutchinsons, Inc., Orleans, MA

ABCDEFGHIJ-DO-86543
First printing, June 1983

THE
EDDIE BAUER
OUTDOOR LIBRARY

Eddie Bauer has been serving the needs of outdoor enthusiasts for three generations. Since 1920, we have been dedicated to developing, testing, and manufacturing the finest in apparel and gear for outdoor adventures. Our aim has been to make outdoor adventures more enjoyable.

Now, sixty-three years after we began, we are answering the needs of another generation of outdoor activists. **Eddie Bauer** Outdoor Guides like this one on Backpacking will help newcomers get started. Others contain up-to-date, tested information to make your outdoor excursions safe, warm, dry, and comfortable.

CONTENTS

ACKNOWLEDGMENTS

Several persons were very helpful in preparing the manuscript for this book, all members of the Eddie Bauer, Inc., staff. Abbie Anderson took over in mid-manuscript stage and smoothed the way for it to be completed. John Kime, a longtime editor on the staff, is a quick, firm, and thorough editor. Bob Murphy was helpful in all stages, especially the chapter dealing with insulation. Jim Wheat helped keep the manuscript honest in all aspects, especially relating to environmental concerns. All were insistent that the book be unbiased and useful to all outdoors people, not just those who are or might be customers of the company.

In addition to this expert help, I relied on several books, periodicals, and pamphlets for information. These include:

Books

Survival With Style by Bradford Angier. Washington and Harrisburg, Pennsylvania: National Wildlife Federation and Stackpole Books, 1972.
Survival in the Outdoors by Byron Dalrymple. New York: Outdoor Life and E.P. Dutton & Co., 1972.
Hiking Light by Marlyn Doan. Seattle: The Mountaineers, 1982.
The New Complete Walker by Colin Fletcher. New York: Alfred A. Knopf, 1974.
Map and Compass by Bjorn Kjellstrom. New York: Charles Scribner's Sons, 1976.
Backpacking: One Step At a Time by Harvey Manning. Seattle: Recreational Equipment, 1972.
The L.L. Bean Guide to the Outdoors by Bill Riviere. New York: Random House, 1981.
The Best About Backpacking by Denise Van Lear, ed. San Francisco: The Sierra Club, 1974.

Periodicals

Outside. Mariah Publications. 1165 N. Clark St., Chicago, Illinois 60610.
Backpacker. Ziff-Davis Publishing Co., One Park Ave., New York 10016.

In addition, I was given access to numerous pamphlets prepared by the outdoor outfitting industry that explain the various fabrics and insulations.

For much of the outdoor etiquette, I am indebted to Cort Green for sharing his vast library of pamphlets, brochures, and other material he has collected over a lifetime of hiking and sailing.

—Archie Satterfield

FOREWORD

In "the good old days," starting at age five for me, we backpacked when there was no other way to transport burdens. Even our dogs backpacked 25 percent of their weight, and they seemed to enjoy it.

When "dudes" chanced our way during fair weather months, wearing laced-leg pants, high lace-up boots and felt hats, they'd rest their packs, wipe their brows, take out their cameras and take pictures of us wearing our bib overalls, buckskin moccasins and perhaps a John Deere give-away advertising cap.

Unlike today, there was an abundance of fuel, fish, wildlife and clean water so we enjoyed good fresh food and the comfort of campfires as well as soft, warm mattresses and lean-to shelters of nature's materials. Our heaviest burdens were packing game or wild berries back home.

One can still enjoy such outings in the remote wilderness areas of North America, such as: Alaska, Western Canada and the primitive areas of Idaho. For the most part, however, all this has changed. Population growth, industrialization, rapid transportation and pollution continue to cause great concern to all who love nature in its natural state. So the well-traveled trails enjoyed by our millions of recreational backpackers must have strict rules and regulations.

I have enjoyed my long career of outdoor outfitting, the many fine people we have served and the part we have played in creating new and better products whenever there came a need.

Today, there is a need for this **Guide to Backpacking**.

I am sure you will find it interesting and well worth owning.

Eddie Bauer

PART I
INTO THE
GREAT
OUTDOORS

THE JOYS OF BACKPACKING

It is late spring and you've put away your cross-country skis for another season because all the snow has gone from the lower elevations. The snow is still high in the hills, but rotten, covered with a sheet of crust. Avalanche lillies are beginning to poke their way up through the porous, granular stuff that hardly resembles snow.

While you wait for good backpacking conditions to come, you put your tent up in the family room or garage to air it out, check it for pinprick holes in the floor, make a few minor repairs and apply a new coat of seam sealer. More than any other piece of backpacking equipment, that tent brings you a keen sense of anticipation.

Next you check the cooking equipment—the packstove and fuel bottles. You burn part of a tank of fuel. Even though you cleaned all your cookware before storing it last fall, you still feel better by putting them through the dishwasher one more time. Your supply of freeze-dried food needs replenishing, and you make a note to test a package of the newest product on the market; you remember the last time you tried some freeze-dried dessert that tasted like flavored cotton.

You repeat the process with your pack, checking it for worn spots, or tears, or a seam that shows signs of extreme wear. Then you check your boots, your first-aid kit, your backpacking clothing (they would be disreputable at an office picnic but they're just fine on the trail).

When you have gone through the entire checklist of backpacking equipment, and repaired and replenished everything, then you start reading the weather forecasts a little more closely and finding various ways to fight off the impatience you always feel during this awkward between-time each year: when it is warm enough for backpacking, but the snow lingers in the mountains and the spring weather remains unpredictable—cold and blowing one day, shirt-sleeve weather the next.

By the time the long Memorial Day weekend comes, you already have your pack loaded and standing in a corner by the door or lying on the workbench in the garage, everything ready and waiting for you to come home, change clothes, and leave. You have probably already slung the pack on a few times, both to get the feel of the load again and simply for nostalgia's sake. The simple act of loading the pack onto your shoulders, snugging in the hipbelt and adjusting the shoulder straps is enough to make you totally ignore any memories of discomfort. Instead, your memory insists

on replaying those great moments from seasons past that have given you a wonderful storehouse of experiences from which to draw when you are house- or office-bound.

At last the first backpacking weekend arrives. If your place of work doesn't have a rigid dress code, you will probably wear your "good" hiking clothes to work that day so you can leave directly from there. If your boss or partner is understanding, you'll leave early on Friday afternoon (they know your heart won't be in your work anyway) so you can beat the traffic out of town. All day you've been wondering if your family or your hiking friends will be ready on time, or if someone will remember at the last minute that one of the children has a dental appointment that afternoon, or that the car's alternator, which has been getting stubborn lately, will choose this time to retire permanently.

Once you and your companions are together in the same vehicle, you start through the community checklist to make sure that each of you didn't assume everyone else would bring a

stove, or that somebody forgot to bring their boots, of all things. So, with impatience growing, you read through the checklist aloud again, checking each other and hoping with religious fervor that everything is there. Better to do this now, you've learned through experience, than to hear that too-common lament, "I thought **you** were bringing the spare tarp!"

The journey to the trailhead is always a repeat of the trip across the Great Plains by Oregon Trail veterans; the cool Rockies with all their fresh water and game are always farther away than they seem. A child echoes your thoughts perfectly: "Aren't we ever going to get there?" Conversely, when you return home, you are always surprised at how close the trailhead really is to your house or apartment.

When you arrive at the trailhead and have left a note with the ranger (if applicable), conversation suddenly seems superfluous as each of you subconsciously prepare for the silence of the trail. Little is said as you unload your packs from the car, lock it, and hoist the packs onto your shoulders.

as well as it did last year. Your boot laces will undoubtedly come untied, or be too tight, and you find your wool shirt is warmer than you really need this time of day.

But with less than a mile between you and your car, you have all these problems solved and you're back in the same mental status you were last fall on the last hike. You know the wait

and anticipation were worth it. And unless you have no choice but to stop soon after leaving, you want to have the trailhead parking lot well out of sight before you find a log for a perch while making these adjustments.

You reach the first night's camp before dark with enough time to pitch the tents, fluff out the sleeping bags,

The first few minutes are always the most difficult on that first hike. You start up the trail with the vague feeling that you've left something behind. The shoulder straps are never quite right, and the hipbelt doesn't seem to ride

Whenever you are hiking a trail that has a signup sheet at the trailhead, fill out the forms (they're often on the honor system) and check out again when you leave the trail at trip's end. Not only are you letting the rangers know who you are and how many are in your party, you are also letting the ranger know you're there in case of an emergency back home.

and get the evening meal going. After carrying a heavy load into camp, you feel so light of foot that you imagine doing a few high jumps with no effort. The standard joke around camp is to eat lots so you won't have so much to carry tomorrow.

If you are in an area where camp-fires are permitted, you build one for the psychological comfort it provides, not necessarily for cooking or even warmth. The cooking is all done over a packstove anyway.

If you are hiking with experienced backpackers, you note how smoothly and quickly the camp chores are disposed of. One team erects the tents, another takes care of the food, while still a third forages for firewood and water, and puts the final touches on the temporary home. Often these chores are performed with no formal division of labor; you see what needs to be done and do it, and with a minimum of conversation; that usually waits until during the evening meal and afterward.

Only after you take off your clothes and slip into your sleeping bag are you fully aware of the deep silence of the wilderness, and you savor it so much that you are reluctant to change positions on your foam pad for fear the slightest rustling sound will destroy the moment. Your last thoughts before going to sleep are of the pleasures of tomorrow, the first full day of back-packing ahead of you. If you are already familiar with the route, you imagine hiking over the entire trail as you drop off to sleep.

This first hike of the season is an important one for you because it can well set the tone of your entire hiking season. The memories of this hike will remain with you and your companions throughout the year, and if it is especially memorable for any reason, you may remember it the rest of your life. If you have youngsters along, or a first-time backpacker, it is important that the hike be neither too strenuous nor too bland. It should be in a beautiful area, and one that isn't so well-used that federal rangers are needed to direct traffic.

The first morning of a trip is always pleasurable—most of the trip is still ahead, and you will have enough fine-tuning adjustments to make on your equipment and psychological adjustments among your companions that you may find yourself spending more time around the breakfast fire than planned. Your start may be delayed an hour or two as you establish the routine of breaking camp and leaving no traces of your visit.

When you are at last on the trail again, you have a few more minor adjustments to make, especially the pace of the hike and the frequency of stops. In every group of two or more there are those who want to "make miles" and those who want to stop and examine wildflowers, watch butterflies, or listen to bird calls. Thus, the length of hiking each day must leave allowances for these varied interests. Indeed, you might best clarify these factors before leaving on the hike, if at all possible. It is better to avoid

backpacking with someone whose interests are very different than to have one person who urges the group ahead while another continually finds something fascinating every ten steps.

If you have planned your trip well, and if the Ferdinands in your group haven't spent too much time sniffing flowers, you arrive at that night's campsite well before darkness falls, allowing plenty of time for resting, strolling around the area, getting your all-important "alone-time" away from the group, and still having sufficient time to prepare the evening meal before dark. By now you are several miles into the wilderness—perhaps the only trace of civilization you can see is the contrail of a high-altitude jet or a manmade satellite winking and whirling its way around Earth like a speeding star.

On the trail it is the simple, basic things that fascinate you as they never do in the city or suburbia. The trembling of a leaf in the breeze has an almost hypnotic effect, as does the sound of that breeze high in the trees. You marvel at the natural designs in the forest—the placing of trees so that each has sufficient space in which to grow. The moss and lichen on rocks, the course a stream has set for itself, the texture of bark, the game trail that meanders along the hillside following the path of least resistance, the placement of wildflowers along the trail and up the hillsides: all these things can intrigue you and take up more of your time than you would ever suspect. Anyone bored on a backpacking trip through the wilderness would be bored in the corner candy store.

By the second or third day of a season's initial trip you'll also have learned a lot about your own body,

A good way to divide camp chores is to break the group into teams. While one team erects tents, another prepares food; one can provide water and the other firewood and fires (where fires are permitted).

your conditioning, and how to parcel out your energy so that you are able to hike with a load on your back for mile after mile, hour after hour, without expending all your energy in one fast-paced sprint. If you are in good health and good physical condition, you can backpack all day long, day after day, at your own comfortable pace, and not become overly fatigued. Stops to admire the scenery, occasional snacks of high-energy foods such as chocolate bars and the so-called trail foods of nuts, raisins, and candy (gorp), all keep your body's fuel supply adequate for the task.

When you finish this first outing of the year back at the trailhead, sweaty and perhaps a bit smelly, tired and even a little sore from the hipbelt and shoulder straps, you will think that the greatest feeling in the world is stowing

the pack in the car and walking around the area without a load on your back. But already you are planning the next trip, making mental notes of what to leave out of the pack the next time, what kind of food or clothing you must have or can live without.

And you will remember: evenings in camp with the conversation dying to a placid silence, the high open ridge you crossed where the wind had blown the plant life flat against the ground, the good physical feeling of striding along the trail with a heavy load on your back as your legs and lungs gained endurance each day, the anticipation each morning for the day's adventures, large and small.

Although you know that many backpackers have been along that route before, and many more will follow, still you return home with a sense

of discovery. You know that you can never hike all the beautiful trails, sleep in all the beautiful meadows, drink from every pure stream, or see the sunsets from every high elevation in any one national forest or national park. But after this first hike of the season is ended, you vow to be very se-

lective in the remaining trails you will be allotted during your life. You know that some may not be as spectacular as the one you've just hiked, but you don't want them to be less interesting, less challenging, or less beautiful.

CHAPTER 1

THE BACKPACKING REVOLUTION

Backpacking as a form of mass recreation is so new that many people assume it was invented at roughly the same time jet engines were installed in commercial aircraft. But they forget that mankind has been involved in various forms of backpacking since he started walking erect and traveling from place to place in search of food and safety. History is replete with wanderers who slung their necessary belongings on their shoulders and back, and struck out across the land in search of something. These early forms of backpacking would not be tolerated today by even the most dedicated walker. Instead of straps, they used thongs made of whatever happened to be available. Their packs were often their bedrolls with their clothing and tools rolled into the bedding.

Native Americans carried their children in a form of backpack, usually part of their parkas or coats. The inventive ones trained dogs to pull parallel sticks—**travois**—with belongings strapped to the sticks. After the Spanish brought horses to the New World, the Indians had a new and more efficient form of transportation, and like people throughout the world, came to think of walking as a form of abject poverty. A family that could not afford a horse to carry them and their belongings was indeed an impoverished family.

Except for the few eccentrics that every society spawns, such as wandering writers and singers, no normal American would think of carrying a load on his or her back when wheeled vehicles—first horse-drawn wagons,

then trains, and finally the automobile—were available for such things. Walking and carrying a load for its own sake was considered silly. In those early days of modern transportation, the wagons, trains, and early automobiles moved slowly enough to see the countryside as one cruised by, and if one had to leave the beaten path, horses were the accepted mode of transportation overland.

But technology does not stand still, and improvements in vehicles were equated with speed. Soon people were being shot across the landscape at such great speeds that the scenery became a blur. Highways and railroads took the path of least resistance, which often meant the most bland scenery. Airplanes flew higher and higher until they crossed the continent above the clouds, so you could get on a plane in New York, fly across the entire continent to Los Angeles, and see only cloud formations. Even in clear weather, scenery from a jet is little more than a flattened bas-relief map.

As always, there remained a few individuals who refused to hurry. When they left home, they wanted to **see** the land they crossed. They wanted to hear cows lowing, see bees and butterflies, smell fresh-cut hay, taste pure mountain stream water, and when they bedded down for the night they wanted to see the starry sky.

This type of traveler had always been with us. In some societies walking was not merely an accepted form of transportation; it was quite common in Europe and far-flung places like New Zealand and Australia. Until well into this century walking was a popular way to see Europe. The British thought nothing of walking for days on end and staying either in inns or in homes, which were the forerunners of the popular bed-and-breakfast establishments now found all over North America today.

But not in America, where the car was almost as important as land ownership, and where religious leaders have had to build drive-in churches in a compromise with car owners; if they wouldn't leave their cars for religious services, then religion would have to meet them at least halfway.

Sometime around World War II this love affair with vehicles reached the point of saturation, something like eating a whole box of chocolates at one sitting. Although few Americans sold their cars and went everywhere on foot, still the time was ripe for an alternate form of recreation.

Again, part of this coming revolution against riding everywhere was partly a result of technology. The Boy Scouts had made a great impression on many Americans who in their adulthood remembered with fondness those overnight hikes. Even though the Boy Scout-era outdoor equipment was quite primitive by contemporary standards—packs painful to carry, tents that weighed no less than 12 pounds, off-the-shelf canned food—still the woodsman mystique stayed with thousands of Americans who earned their livings in cities.

World War II made a considerable difference in many products. Air-

and dehydrated foods have become so common that hardly a bag of groceries leaves the store today without at least one item of these processed soups or additives in the sack. And again, the greatest savings are in weight and bulk.

Now with the necessities of backpacking reduced in weight and bulk, the time was right for ways to make use of these products. When World War

Backpacks in the 1920-1930 era were made of wood, cord, webbing, and canvas—primitive by contemporary standards.

craft-type aluminum made it possible to build backframes of a metal that was as light as it was strong. Plastic, which was languishing before the war, soon became a perfectly acceptable substitute for goods formerly made of leather, canvas, cotton, and metal. And it, too, was lightweight. Foods were revolutionized. Gone were the trips where canned pork and beans were the mainstay of campers. Freeze-dried

II ended, still another revolution was in progress, this one involving a natural product: goose down.

Only a few years before the war, Eddie Bauer had taken out a patent on the first quilted goose-down coat. Few articles of clothing have so revolutionized America's dressing habits. These quilted designs were so efficient and attractive they were destined to become fashionable for casual wear.

When the war broke out, Eddie Bauer designed flying suits for the Air Corps that were far superior to any available anywhere in the world. Not only were they lightweight, they were also more flexible than other designs; they kept plane crews comfortable at the high altitudes even with bomb bay and gun turret doors open.

When the war ended, Eddie Bauer turned this expertise to the civilian outdoor market. He designed new types of coats and insulated pants, and also sleeping bags with sophisticated baffling systems to keep the down from shifting.

With all these ingredients—lightweight gear, convenient food, and down clothing—America was ready for the backpacking revolution when it came.

And come it did. These dedicated people did not combine backpacking with other activities, such as hunting, fishing, or trapping. They walked with their food, clothing, and shelter on their backs for the simple joy of backpacking. Their only purpose was to walk trails, eat and sleep outside, then walk back to the trailheads, and go home. Walking became a form of pleasure **in itself** rather than a means of making a journey. The journey became the goal.

Once this form of recreation became established—and it became established very quickly—most manufacturers were not prepared. Even though the technology for lightweight, durable equipment was available, it was some time before production and design could match with the demand. So backpackers had to make do with what was available or to create their own equipment. Backpackers took to drying their own

food, making jerky, mixing trail foods, haunting military surplus stores, and sewing their own clothing and tents. And then the new materials began to appear on the market: all lightweight; because if backpackers are fanatical about anything, it is weight.

Coinciding with this explosion of backpacking was the increasing awareness of wilderness values. The postwar boom in industry created a need for more hydroelectric power, which in turn meant more wild rivers turned into pools of slackwater behind dams, covering valleys and even towns. The boom meant more and more timber being cut from the mountainsides, more logging roads, more highways, more mining, more waste products discharged into the air and the streams.

By the early 1960s environmental lines had been drawn: it was the environmentalists against the industrialists. And most of the former were backpackers. It doesn't necessarily follow that most backpackers were outspoken environmental preservationists, but they were at least likely candidates for anti-industrial lobbying, because the things they liked the most—natural beauty and clean air and water—were being threatened.

By another decade, backpacking had grown to become one of **the** most popular forms of outdoor recreation, and its practitioners came from virtually every segment of life. Before the 1980s arrived, there were increasing and new concerns for the wilderness backpackers love so well: if anything, the wilderness areas were now being loved to the point of destruction. Trails were so well-used that they often turned into gullies. Well-meaning campers were causing irreparable damage by

Use radios

Build fires against trees

DON'TS OF CAMPING

Pick wild-flowers

Over-use trails

Feed animals

Take firewood from living trees

Leave garbage or smouldering fires

Let pack animals damage environment

burning all of the downed timber and branches—and often felling young trees—for their campfires. What they didn't burn, they used for tent poles, for bedding, and a host of other purposes. Trees were killed by fires built around their root systems. Pack animals were allowed to forage to a destructive extent.

It became apparent before the 1980s arrived that not only should backpackers be concerned with lightweight equipment, they must be as equally concerned with the light touch in the wilderness. Older slogans such as "Leave only your footprints behind" had to be discarded: too many footprints **were** being left behind.

Still, of all the sports North Americans have become addicted to, backpacking is clearly one sport that will always be with us. It is a textbook example of the lifetime sports concept, as opposed to team sports that are reserved for the young. Youngsters and octogenarians are found on trails all over the continent, each enjoying the simple art of walking and each doing so on their own terms because backpacking is perhaps the most versatile of all sports. You can do it at your own pace and under your own terms as long as you can walk.

Because of all the emphasis in recent years on wilderness travel and environmental concerns, hiking and backpacking have come to be thought of as only wilderness travel. Forgotten are those day hikes from one train depot across country to the next, or circular walking tours through the countryside that can be completed in a single day (or in several days with a small knapsack). Not all hiking trips need be major expeditions requiring sixty or more pounds on your back. Instead, you can carry a small knapsack to hold a change of clothing, a few snack items, and perhaps a book or two, while you hike from village to village, staying in inns or bed-and-breakfast establishments. This is a form of travel and recreation largely forgotten in North America, but still very popular in Europe. It can easily be revived in more densely populated parts of North America where towns and villages are only a few miles apart. In the less populated West, it is a bit more difficult to travel on foot without your housing and bedding on your back.

Thus, hiking and backpacking need not be equated solely with wilderness. It can be done anywhere you choose to do it.

CHAPTER 2

ESPECIALLY FOR FIRST-TIMERS

Now that you have read something of the history of backpacking, and of the pleasures it offers, suppose that you have lived a totally urban life and have carried nothing on your back except possibly a child, hiked no farther than the bus stop or subway station, that the only fire you've cooked over was marshmallows in a fireplace, and the only time you've seen a wilderness is from an airplane at 30,000 feet.

Now what?

Although millions of Americans are at least vaguely familiar with hiking and backpacking, millions of others are not at all. Chances are that novices are a bit put off when they first approach an experienced back-packer because the sport has its own jargon and mystique. The beginner is made to feel he or she must serve out an apprenticeship before being able to participate on an equal basis with the veterans.

The best way to approach this sport is the way you would approach anything else new. The fact that you are reading this book is a step in the right direction, of course. Next you should read others. Every region of North America has its own particular requirements for enjoyable backpacking. Your needs for desert hiking are quite different from those in New England, and the Rockies have still other requirements. While the same basic equipment is sufficient for all regions, still there are differences: some subtle, some dramatic. For example, cotton

is far superior to wool for desert hiking (except for a warm shirt or sweater at night); while in the areas where both cold and dampness are common, you should reverse the process and have everything woolen except perhaps a cotton shirt or jeans for those warm afternoons.

After you have studied the new sport exhaustively, both in general terms and in the particular needs of your region, you should next consider joining an organization that promotes backpacking, such as the Big Six of backpacking: The Adirondack, Appalachian, and Green Mountain clubs in the East; the Mazamas, Mountaineers, and Sierra clubs in the West. While each of these clubs has a strong environmental-protection bent, you don't have to sign a pledge to picket to belong.

Other choices are local YMCA and YWCA organizations, community colleges, and similar groups.

Another preparatory activity is buying several topographical maps of your area and studying them along

with local guidebooks for backpackers. One good way to select those initial backpacking routes is to read the guidebook descriptions of them while following the route on the topographical map. In most parts of North America you can find suitable backpacking areas within a two- or three-hour drive from your home.

Once you have gone this far—but have not left town yet—you should sign on with a group, or go with friends, on a trial outing. Rent or borrow the basic equipment—backpack, tent, and sleeping bag, if you don't own them—and try a weekend or four-day trip that isn't a forced march through the wilderness and over ridge and valley. Some backpackers equate mileage with pleasure and treat trails almost as interstate highways, chugging along at a fast clip in order to get "there." Others are amblers who don't care if they hike two or ten miles; being there is the main pleasure.

If you have led a rather sedentary life, that first trip—and perhaps the next one or two—aren't going to be as comfortable as the clothing and pack advertisements make backpacking seem. If you are carrying a full load you are going to feel awkward and off-balance when the pack is first on your back. And until you get the hang of adjusting the straps, it is going to feel uncomfortable as well. You'll hardly be able to restrain yourself from uttering the old chestnut about pain: "It feels so good when it stops."

But after a few minutes, and a few miles, you will not only be able to tolerate that unnatural burden on your back, you start enjoying the general good, physical feeling that comes with exercise in beautiful, interesting surroundings. And before long you will be quite emotionally attached to that pack and your other equipment—especially your boots, if you've chosen them carefully—and you will wonder why you waited so long to take up this sport.

That pack, alternately cursed and blessed by all backpackers, is your complete home. It has your food, clothing, shelter, medicine cabinet, recreational equipment such as books and games, plus chocolate and nuts and other items to satisfy your gastronomical urges. Thus, you become quite attached to your pack; you will be glad somebody invented one with all those nifty pockets for munchies and maps because it enables you to get out into the wilderness without having to hurry home before dark. It also lets you choose your own routes for trips of varying lengths, because you can carry enough in your pack to live at

least a week, two or three weeks if you are especially strong.

To repeat, the freedom of movement backpacking provides is its strongest argument. But backpacks are always uncomfortable, you say? Nonsense. Even a $50,000 automobile is uncomfortable after a few hours of driving.

Now that we've totally convinced you that backpacking is the sport for you—we **have** convinced you, haven't we?—we will press onward with further discussion on getting started.

If you go about acquiring clothing and equipment in a cautious, unhurried, and systematic manner, you can buy gear now that will still be perfectly usable when your children (and even their children) take up the sport. The best equipment is durable and

CONDITIONING

Most backpackers are the kind of people who stay in reasonably good condition throughout the year; backpacking in the summer, skiing in the winter, and some other form or exercise such as swimming, running, or team sports regularly.

However, there appears to be no adequate substitute for conditioning before backpacking trips than putting on a pack with a normal load and taking off on warmup hikes early in the season. It isn't unusual to see people with packs on walking and jogging trails in the spring, getting accustomed to the extra load and building up the muscles that are called into service with the heavier load.

An alternative is working out with weights, but it is only second-best to going on day hikes with a loaded pack and then stretching them out into eight- and ten-mile hikes as your conditioning improves.

Another choice is to make your first few backpacking trips short in mileage, then gradually work into the longer trips.

built to last, from down garments and woolen shirts to tents and packs. With proper treatment, your packstove will last for generations, requiring only an occasional replacement of working parts such as fuel caps, pumps, and wicks. Sure, it will begin looking disreputable after a few years with all its nicks, bumps, and scratches, but it will continue working just the same.

The high-quality goose-down parka or sleeping bag you buy today will last the rest of your life with the proper care and cleaning. The fabric containing the down may eventually wear out and have to be replaced

DOGS

One of the first questions apartment owners and wilderness rangers are asked by families is whether dogs are permitted. The answer is increasingly negative in all wilderness areas, for very good reasons, in spite of their owners' love for them.

Dogs are a bother to other hikers and nearly all forms of wildlife. They are usually noisy, are likely to steal food wherever they can find it, are inclined to lift their legs against anything that doesn't move, fight with other dogs, and scare the socks off backpackers if the dog is larger than a dachshund.

With this broadside in mind, there are some areas that do permit dogs to mingle with backpackers, particularly private land and areas managed by agencies other than the Forest Service and National Park Service. Many families feel quite lost without their pets, and not all pets are pests to others.

Here are some of the characteristics of a nice trail doggy:

- They are kept on a leash on the trail so they won't startle other backpackers, and they do not wander away from the immediate campsite. If they tend to wander, they are put on a long leash at camp.
- They do not bark.
- They do not bite.
- If they use the trail for a bathroom, you immediately remove the evidence.
- If another dog appears, you restrain your animal and ask the other owner to do the same.
- If the trail is shared with pack animals, you always restrain your dog when meeting a packstring or riders.

What if you are a pet hater and are sharing a trail or campground with one or more dogs? You are stuck with it and had as well make the best of it. Dogs are quick to recognize hostility or fear, so stay as far away from the animal as possible. If it isn't restrained, count to 10 or 100 or however far it takes you to simmer down, then politely discuss the matter with the owners.

The next time you go backpacking, choose a place where pets are not permitted.

after you've patched it too many times, but the down itself will last for decades or generations. It can be salvaged when the bag material wears out and used in other sleeping bags, in pillows, or in comforters or parkas you make yourself.

Tents are equally durable provided they are not abused by being pitched without a ground cloth beneath them, or over sharp objects that poke holes in the floor. If small holes are kept repaired, the seams sealed against leaks, and repairs made as needed, and if the fabric is protected from the bright sun, tents will last many seasons without showing signs of use. Many last a decade, some two decades.

In short, by shopping wisely, many of your backpacking purchases will be one-time purchases. They will likely outlive you. After your first investments, repairs on your boots and replacement of small parts on your stove, and other similar housekeeping items will be the extent of your costs each spring when the backpacking season begins.

Leash your dog if you must take it along.

PART II
GETTING
READY

CHAPTER 3

THE QUESTION OF WEIGHT

Backpackers are preoccupied by a number of subjects—their feet, their backs, trail conditions, encroaching civilization, crowded wilderness areas, ad infinitum—but weight of equipment continues to be **the** primary concern of all who carry their home on their back for any length of time. Formulas galore have been devised to tell us how much of a load we should be able to carry in comfort, and they usually are based on our total body weight.

Some backpackers of a scientific bent compute the weight of a loaded pack down to ounces and will buy a three-bladed pocket knife instead of one with four blades to save an ounce or less. Weight can become an obsession. It can lead you into the temp-

tation to eat two days' rations the first day out just to lighten the load. In the early years of backpacking, it wasn't unusual to find items such as hatchets, big knives, and even articles of clothing discarded along trails. Weight, obviously, is the major factor in this form of recreation.

Gradually, over the years, the weight was reduced: nylon replaced treated cotton for tents; down replaced cotton and wool for sleeping gear, followed by synthetics that do not absorb moisture; aluminum replaced steel in packframes and cooking equipment; and freeze-dried and dehydrated foods replaced canned and unprocessed foods.

Until only recently, many backpackers assumed that the minimums

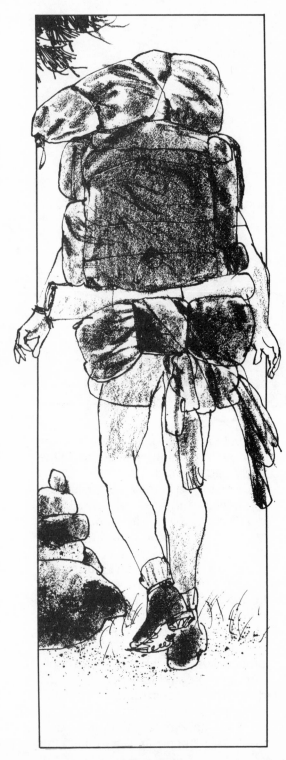

in weight had been reached. It was taken for granted that sturdy hiking boots had to weigh five or more pounds and that a pack loaded for a week-long hike would weigh at least 50 pounds, often more.

But that has changed, and the newest topic of conversation among backpackers is the ultralight equipment just being introduced on the market as this is being written.

This new equipment means that a fully-loaded pack can weigh between 20 and 30 pounds!

It means a tent will weigh less than five pounds, a sleeping bag around two pounds, the pack itself only one pound, a two-piece rainsuit less than a pound, and boots with Vibram soles a pound—give or take two or three ounces either way depending on size.

With this new equipment comes a refinement of an old concept of taking only what you need and making certain your equipment and clothing are versatile. Some call it "functional redundancy," meaning that each item you wear or carry should have more than one use, sometimes several.

Some examples of new products and new approaches to using them are described in this chapter.

SHELTER

More and more the word "shelter" is used instead of tent or tarp, in part because newer tents are often little more than shaped tarps or raingear. Some models are so versatile that they can be called lightweight bivouac bags that keep the ground moisture, dew, or rain off you while you sleep. Some can be inserted into your sleeping bag as a moisture barrier between you and your bag, keeping perspiration from entering your bag's insulation.

A poncho is one of the more versatile pieces of clothing you will carry because it can be used as raingear to protect you and your pack, as a tent or shelter, as a groundcloth beneath your tent or bivouac bag, as a tarp over your cooking area, and even as a liner inside your bag for the moisture barrier mentioned above. Thus, a poncho is raingear, tent, tarp, liner, groundcloth—all in one piece of clothing that can weigh as little as eight to ten ounces.

Bivouac shelters come in a variety of types: the most popular have two lightweight fiberglass or aluminum wands to make them form a low-profile shelter. Some have zippered openings with insect netting over one end for your head, and there is a rainfly to cover the netting. Gore-Tex is a popular material for these shelters since it is at once waterproof and breathable. These "bivy" bags or sacks weigh less than three pounds.

Full-sized tents made of the new generation of ultralight materials (usually spinnaker cloth or nylon taffeta) weigh in from three pounds for a crowded sleeping capacity for two upward to less than seven pounds for three persons. By spreading the weight between each person sleeping in them, nobody carries more than three pounds for shelter.

SLEEPING BAGS

A sleeping bag is one of the most difficult items to buy because most backpackers are out in a wide range of temperatures, from well below zero to over 100° F. Few sleeping bags have a comfort range of more than 40° F at the most, and that stretches your luck.

The alternative is to treat sleeping bags much as you do clothing: instead of dressing in layers, you prepare your bed in layers. By buying a sleeping bag that is lightweight and suited for mild temperatures, you have the foundation of a sleeping system. You can extend the range downward by wearing warm, dry (it must be dry) clothing inside the bag, such as a down coat or sweater, woolen pants and socks, and woolen cap.

Another method of extending the range is to buy a liner for the bag that will extend the range by as much as 20° while adding very little weight.

And another, as discussed earlier, is to use a poncho as a liner and vapor barrier to help reflect heat back onto your body instead of letting it escape through the bag.

For this lightweight concept, goose down is still the best insulation because it is the lightest available; it is also the most compressible of all forms of insulation. Remember: bulk is almost as much a problem as weight.

New types of insulation are still being developed, some of which are quite successful in offering alternatives to down. Some synthetics (many avid students of the sport call them "hydrocarbon honkers" because they substitute for goose down) have almost matched down in both weight and bulk, but not yet. Their major advantage is that they can get wet and still provide insulation after being wrung out, whereas down cannot be wrung out and must be dried slowly and carefully.

More on these types of insulation later.

PACKS

Because the contents of packs weigh considerably less than the 50-pound or more loads in conventional backpacking, the packs themselves now do not need to be built as strong as bridge trusses. Consequently, much of the weight savings can be accomplished in the packs themselves.

Conventional packs have two major components: the frame, usually aircraft-quality aluminum, and the bag that attaches to the frame.

Ultralight packs combine these elements into one complete system. The framework, if it can be called that, is built into the pack itself, so that all you have is a bag with shoulder straps and a hipbelt. More or less. They are designed to ride on the natural contours of the human back with padding in the appropriate places, so that the 20- to 30-pound load is supported by the shoulders, hips, and the back itself.

The straps are easily adjustable, so that when you walk on more or less

level terrain your shoulders and hips support the load; and you can make almost endless adjustments to shift the burden back and forth between the two carrying points to avoid fatigue. Then when you begin a hard climb, the weight can be placed on the back by cinching the straps more tightly to give you more leg and arm freedom.

BOOTS

Footwear for backpackers has gone through a number of developments—and fads—and all in the past seemed to be based on the irrefutable law that good hiking boots had to be very stiff and certainly very heavy.

Only in the early 1980s has this doctrine been seriously challenged by boots with stiff soles but with pliable and lightweight uppers. The introduction of synthetic materials to replace leather has been largely responsible for this new technology. Waterproof cloth, such as Cordura, and breath-

---

BACKPACKER'S TIP

Boot dryers on the market now resemble boot trees with electrical heating elements in them to give a low, even heat to dry the leather without stiffening or cracking. But what about drying your boots on the trail? Some backpackers have heated gravel or sand in a skillet over the cookstove, then dumped the hot gravel or sand into the boots. They say it works.

able fabrics, such as Gore-Tex, have made a major impact on footwear.

The weight savings are enormous,

BACKPACKER'S TIP

Most parents are aware that when they go on a trip and leave their children behind, they should also leave a signed form giving permission for the children to be treated in case of an emergency. But few think to give the same form to their children under the age of 18 who go on a backpacking trip with friends. Have your family doctor give you a form, or tell you the wording, and have the children carry one with them on all trips.

BACKPACKING EQUIPMENT CHECKLIST

Pack
Survival kit
Plastic tube or bag for emergency use
Tent, poles, pegs
Tent (rain) fly
Sleeping bag
Sleeping bag liner
Waterproof stuff sack
Polyurethane sleeping pad
Ground cover
Nylon cord
Stove
Stove fuel
Stove windshield
Stove base or pad

Ponchos are versatile garments. They can be used as ponchos, ground cover, shelter for sleeping, and for cooking.

Metal grill
Frying pan
Pots or cook kit
Gripper handle for pots
Scouring pad
Eating utensils
Can opener
Foil
Cup
Polybottle
Food and drink
Quick-energy trail snacks
Plastic water bags
Plastic litter bag
Flashlight
Extra flashlight batteries and bulb
Candle
Waterproof matches
Map and compass
Sunglasses
Whistle

Pocket knife
Ground air signals
Needle and thread or sewing kit
Toothbrush, toothpaste
Biodegradable soap
Toilet paper
Other toiletries, as dictated by personal needs
Medical supplies (see separate list)
Safety pins
Sunburn preventive, lip balm
Bug repellent
Water purifier
Paper and pencil
Special ropes and hardware, if you're a climber
Camera and film
Binoculars
Individual preferences, such as books

and wearing sturdy hiking boots is now no more fatiguing than wearing running shoes.

A WORD OF WARNING

The move toward ultralight clothing and equipment is not without its side effects. Responsible salespersons in outfitting stores will warn you that what you gain in weight savings can be offset by packs and tents that wear out rapidly. Toughness and durability have had to yield to weight considerations, so some materials used in these ultralights are flimsy in comparison to the rugged fabrics you may already be accustomed to. A tent that is treated with your usual casual attitude toward the surface of the ground or the pack you let slide down a rock face simply will not hold up if it is made of the ultralight materials.

So when you investigate the ultralights, do so with your own planned uses in mind. For the average backpacker who treats his camping equipment with the same consideration antique china receives, ultralights will be a good investment and will increase enjoyment of backpacking trips considerably.

But if durability and rugged equipment are part of your normal backpacking requirements, then you must be prepared for more frequent equipment replacements.

OTHER CONSIDERATIONS

If you use your backpacking equipment for other sports, such as bicycling, kayaking, or cross-country skiing, ultralight products will be a good investment since weight and compactness are major considerations in these sports, too.

CHAPTER 4

PACKS

Like the mythical search for the lost chord and the golden fleece, backpackers and manufacturers have been searching for the perfect pack for centuries. Various methods of carrying heavy loads have been devised by peoples all over the world. It is little wonder that mankind has always had a great romance with animals of burden and with transport machines, beginning with the wheel.

The search for the perfect pack goes on. Internal and external frames are used. Hipbelts, shoulder straps, and even tumplines (that go around the forehead or the chest from the burden on the back) have been experimented with. Until someone discovers a method of overcoming gravity, people will still have to carry their belongings into the wilderness on their

backs if they want to go alone without pack animals or machinery.

In general, packs are divided into two basic designs: the internal-frame designs and external frames. The external frames are the most common and familiar, and are used for everything from day hikes to expeditions. But internal frames are steadily making inroads because they have a versatility that makes them practical for both light loads and for rugged-country and climbing use. The advantages are that they are close-fitting and are less likely to cause balance problems when the terrain requires you to bend and straighten frequently. The internal-frame packs are particularly popular with climbers and cross-country skiiers, for example.

As noted in the Chapter 1, there

was a time when frames alone weighed almost as much as a fully loaded pack of the new ultralight category. The development of lightweight-yet-strong metals during World War II resulted in aircraft-quality aluminum tubing that has high tensile strength while weighing little. This met-

roughly half as much as aircraft-aluminum frames and have an immunity to bending out of shape while still flexing with body movement. Manufacturers claim they are also stronger than any metal frame.

Still, a pack is essentially a very simple piece of equipment that fol-

If you take a dog on backpacking trips (see comments on dogs in text), it is a good idea to have them carry their own food in packs available for dogs. Of course, the animal should be accustomed to the pack before the trip.

allurgical advance was quickly adopted by the recreation industry at the same time it was utilizing new, strong, lightweight synthetic fibers that could be made into water-repellant fabrics that wore longer than natural fabrics while also weighing less. Both the metal and the fabrics were the basis for the new ultralight pack developments.

Several years passed before the most recent advancements appeared. Now packframes are available made of carbon fibers, particularly graphite. These weigh

lows the curvature of one's spine and is kept in place by straps, two for the shoulders and one for the hips. The obvious way to support the biggest loads with the most comfort is on the hips and shoulders rather than the back, which is one of mankind's weakest spots.

For maximum comfort, the pack should not ride flush against the back without air circulation. The frame should have enough flexibility to bend slightly with the body, rather than hanging there like a block of wood.

Obviously, a pack for a person 5'

tall cannot be expected to fit one who stands 6' or taller—and vice versa. Thus, packs become more and more customized, much like any article of clothing.

Other than certain embellishments, this is the status of the vast majority of packs today. You will find many different designs that offer you conveniences, such as a choice between zippers and closing straps, attachments for spare tools, a wide variety of optional pockets, and a broad selection of materials.

There are day packs, fanny packs, expedition packs, summit packs, and so forth. There are packs that come with three to six compartments, some detachable so you can leave most of the weight in camp while you go off on a day hike with your food, your Ten Essentials, and a few other small items in a fanny pack that attaches to your belt or is held on with a hipbelt.

The variety is wide, limited only by manufacturers' designers. But a typical pack for a three-day or longer trip will have these features:

- Divided compartment so you can separate clothing from food and camp tools.
- Side pockets, up to four, so you can put your toilet articles in one pocket, eating implements in another, flashlight, compass, and similar items in still another. You may want to keep trail food in one pocket, or segregate your stove fuel into its own pocket in case of possible leakage.
- Map flap, usually covering one of the compartments, so you can store your maps flat and in a readily accessible place.
- Extra attachments, such as D-rings or straps to hang extra tools—your ice axe, camera tripod, and so forth.

- Extensions—both on top and bottom—so you can strap your tent or sleeping bag and poly pad.
- The fabric should be at least water-repellent. It should be resistant to abrasion and easy to clean with a damp cloth.
- Pack covers should be used in rain. Most packs are not waterproof; the material needs to "breathe."
- The frame should be flexible, yet strong enough to survive being banged against trees and rocks, yet light enough to lift with one finger. While aircraft-quality aluminum tubing is the most popular material, some forms of flexible yet rugged plastic are also being used successfully.

EDDIE BAUER ON PACKS

"I made my first packboard in 1920, using canvas and a wooden frame. The pack weighed 2$\frac{1}{3}$ pounds and could carry up to 150 pounds in a pinch. Today's aircraft aluminum frame packs are available in varying sizes, adjust for comfort, and can carry heavy loads comfortably."

Packs are the most difficult piece of equipment for the beginning backpacker to accept. Virtually no one carries loads on their backs these days except for the pleasure of backpacking, so the beginner must go through a learning process similar to that of a horse being broken in to saddle or pack. That load just doesn't feel nat-

Packs are designed for load ranges and specific uses:

A. The medium-sized frame pack is good for most two-to four-day hikes. Extensions can sometimes be added to the frames for attaching tents and sleeping bags above and below the sacks.

B. An internal-frame pack is recommended for climbing because it clings closely to the back for greater balance. They are also good for cross-country skiing.

C. A fanny pack is ideal for short day hikes when you want to carry a sweater or raingear, a lunch and, of course, the Ten Essentials. Many fanny packs attach to the main pack.

D. A fully equipped pack that can be used for expeditions of a week or more in duration.

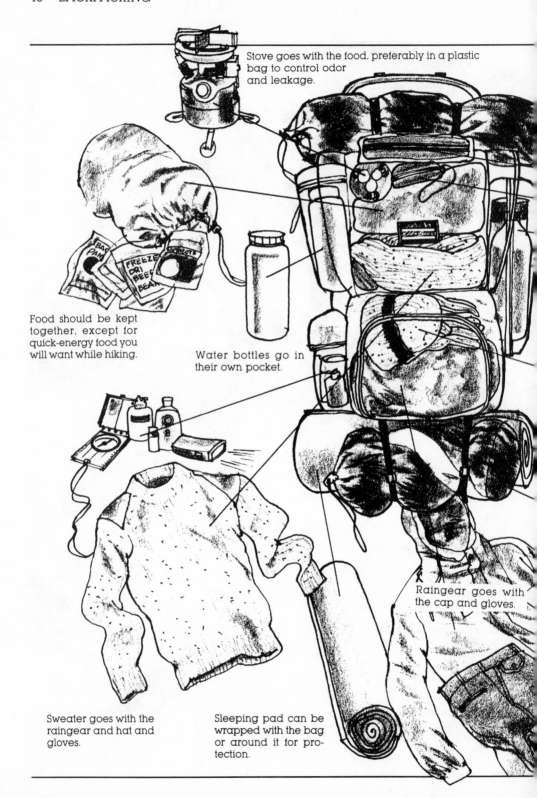

Stove goes with the food, preferably in a plastic bag to control odor and leakage.

Food should be kept together, except for quick-energy food you will want while hiking.

Water bottles go in their own pocket.

Raingear goes with the cap and gloves.

Sweater goes with the raingear and hat and gloves.

Sleeping pad can be wrapped with the bag or around it for protection.

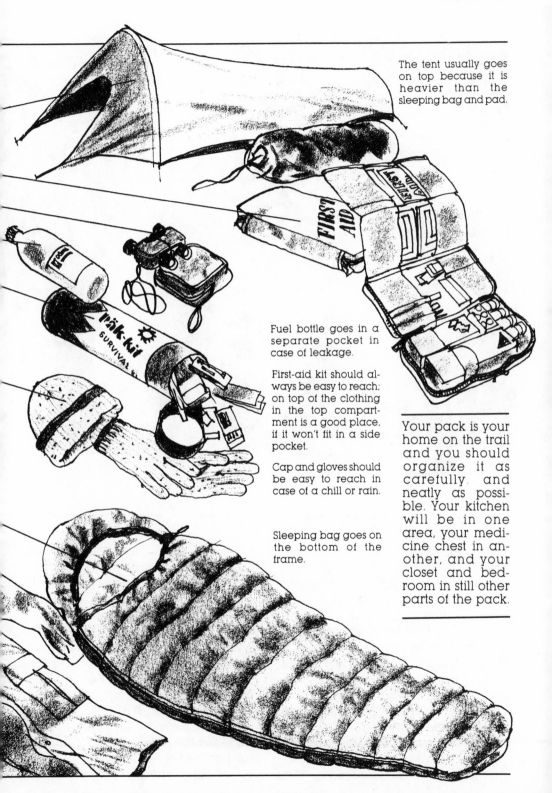

The tent usually goes on top because it is heavier than the sleeping bag and pad.

Fuel bottle goes in a separate pocket in case of leakage.

First-aid kit should always be easy to reach; on top of the clothing in the top compartment is a good place, if it won't fit in a side pocket.

Cap and gloves should be easy to reach in case of a chill or rain.

Sleeping bag goes on the bottom of the frame.

Your pack is your home on the trail and you should organize it as carefully and neatly as possible. Your kitchen will be in one area, your medicine chest in another, and your closet and bedroom in still other parts of the pack.

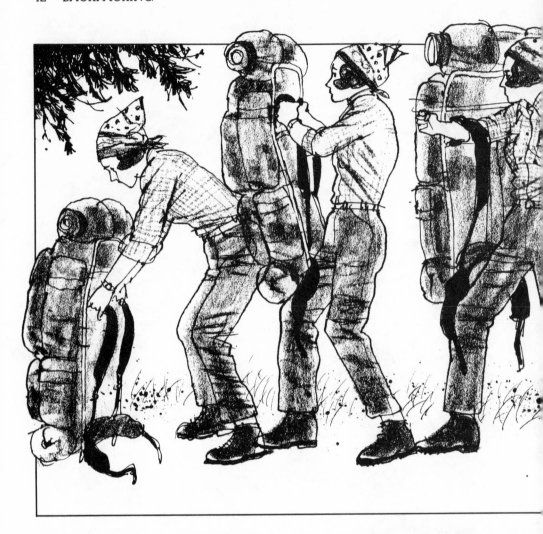

ural back there; and more than one first-timer has uttered the old back-packers' lament that if it hurts, it must be fun. This often happens after the beginner has tried to put the loaded pack on and did an awkward dance worthy of a silent-film star. Then once the pack is on, the unnatural feeling of the pack throws its bearer off balance for several steps. And finally, once it is on properly and balance is restored, the bearer wonders how to get the blasted thing off without just dropping it.

There are various ways of getting the pack on without becoming overly fatigued and grouchy in the process. One way is to lift the pack with both hands—if it isn't too heavy—then slip one arm through the proper shoulder strap, lean forward while shifting the weight to the back, then slip the other arm through the other shoulder strap, and then cinch up the hipbelt. Then adjustments can be made for the best balance of weight by tightening or loosening the shoulder straps and putting the hipbelt in the proper location and at the proper tightness.

Another way is to put the pack on

something nearby, such as a log, stump, table, or rock—and then back into it. If you are fortunate enough to find such a surface, virtually no effort is required.

Another method is the buddy system. You lift the pack onto your partner's back; and your partner returns the favor.

And still another is to hoist the pack, back toward you, onto one knee. Then slip an arm through the shoulder strap, and swing the pack to your back.

Once it is on and you're starting down the trail, you should experiment with several adjustments of the straps and hipbelt until you have the pack in the most comfortable position. And you should change that adjustment occasionally to give your shoulders, back, and hips a rest. While the hipbelt is supposed to rest on the hipbone, change its location occasionally up or down to avoid raising blisters or chafing your skin.

You can also change your walking system from time to time to avoid fatigue. Try leaning a bit further forward for a few yards to rest the weight of the pack flatter on your back.

If you are on level terrain, you can reach behind you with both hands and lift the pack slightly to relieve the strain on your shoulders and hips.

Unless you are an exceptionally strong hiker, or have a very light load, you will want to stop frequently for short breaks. It is best to leave your pack on during these brief stops. The best ones are when you can sit on a log or a rock with the base of the pack resting on the log or rock with no pressure on your shoulders or hips. It takes much more effort to get back into a pack than simply to rest with it still attached gently to you.

When you stop for lunch or for the night's camp, you have several choices of ways to get away from the pack at last. You can do like some irritable hik-

LOADING THE PACK

Although no hard and fast rules can be written about the best way to load packs—each of us likes the load distributed a bit differently—still the majority of backpackers prefer the heavier objects both high in the pack and against the frame (closest to your back). This seems to be the best system of balancing the load and keeping it from tugging away on your hipbelt and shoulder straps.

How you load the other equipment is usually a matter of experimentation. It is a minor source of irritation to have to paw through each side pocket, flap, and compartment to look for something that was there yesterday, but today is mysteriously in your parka pocket.

Thus, you should establish your own method of organizing the pack. The toilet articles can be in one side pocket, eating utensils in another, first-aid kid in still another, and so forth. If nothing else works, get strips of adhesive tape for each pocket and write the contents on them.

Obviously, the things you need for the night's camp can be inside the main compartment or compartments since you won't need them on the trail. Thus, your extra clothing, cooking gear, and food can be in these compartments.

Your tent is usually tied to the top of the pack because it is usually heavier than your sleeping bag and pad. These go to the bottom. Usually. Some packs have lower compartments just right for keeping the sleeping bag out of the weather.

If the sky threatens rain, you should have your raingear at the ready so that you can reach back and pull it out without having to open the pack. The buddy system comes in handy here: it is quicker and neater to help each other with quick changes, such as putting on a poncho and being certain it covers the pack. Of course, the best solution for keeping packs dry is a waterproof packsack that fits over the entire load and ties at the bottom.

Some experimentation will lead you to the loading system that is best for you.

ers and just drop it while you jump out of the way, hoping it doesn't burst and leave you with a load to carry in your arms. So don't do it.

The simplest method is to reverse one of the ways to get into it in the first place. Lean forward with the weight on your back, unbuckle the hipbelt, slip your arms out of the shoulder straps, and ease the pack down on one side of you.

Or back up to a log or a rock and support it there while unbuckling. Or use the buddy system.

It is best to avoid standing a loaded pack against a tree or rock because the weight directly on the bottom of the frame can damage it. Remove the heaviest objects, such as your tent, sleeping bag, and cooking equipment, first. Or better yet, lay the pack flat on the ground or on a log or rock.

Always carry a few spare parts with you, such as the D- or O-rings that keep the pack attached to the frame. Check your pack for signs of wear before each trip, looking for seams beginning to part or unravel, webbing coming loose, or rips or tears.

Thus far we have been discussing the largest model of pack, the external-frame pack that will carry enough food, clothing, and shelter for an expedition. Most dedicated backpackers own one. But there are a variety of other smaller packs intended for specific uses.

RUCKSACKS AND KNAPSACKS

Most of these—they seem to be interchangeable terms—are an intermediate between the fanny packs and external-frame backpacks. They can carry loads up to 40 pounds. However, most backpackers prefer to use them for day hikes or rock climbing trips because they become a true burden with the heavier loads in them.

They are excellent for photographers who want to take several camera bodies and lenses, plus the Ten Essentials, on a day trip. They are also suitable for shorter, overnight hikes because you can cram a sleeping bag and basic shelter, such as a one-man tent or tarp, into them with enough room left over for your food and extra clothing.

They're sometimes called "summit packs" because they can be cinched close to the body while climbing and, therefore, do not affect your balance as a larger pack would.

Some have external frames that are an integral part of the pack. These packs are capable of holding larger loads for trips that, for some reason, are unsuitable for the larger external-frame backpack.

While it is possible to use these rucksacks or knapsacks for longer trips, few backpackers do so because they are constructed for the bulk of the weight to hang from the shoulders— a very wearying situation. In this case, they are a definite second choice.

FANNY PACKS

As noted earlier, many of these small packs are actually one component of the full-sized backpack; such a pack can be removed from the frame and strapped around your waist, or it can beheld on by your belt. A fanny pack will carry food, an article or two of extra clothing, or simply your Ten Essentials.

Unless you always wear a parka with pockets, the fanny pack is the most convenient method for going on short hikes away from your campsite; and you'll find yourself using your fanny pack for jogging, bicycling, or going for a walk with a camera.

CHAPTER 5

SLEEPING BAGS

The search goes on for the perfect insulation in sleeping bags, just as the search continues for a suitable replacement for the best insulation of them all—premium quality northern goose down. Perfection, of course, is both in the eye of the beholder and an impossibility to achieve. But we have never had a wider choice of acceptable insulations than we do at the present.

The first breakthrough in sleeping-bag construction was in 1936, when Eddie Bauer patented the construction of quilted jackets insulated with goose down. This patented process was the first to keep the down from shifting about and was for years the only real advancement made in insulated outdoor gear.

Then, after World War II, came the synthetics that have gradually moved closer and closer to matching the insulating properties of down, as well as down's light weight and ability to be compressed into a small size for carrying or storage. No synthetic has yet been able to match exactly Mother Nature's goose down, but they are getting closer.

They are, however, close enough so that the tradeoffs you must make are lessened with each new generation of synthetic insulations. The advantage of synthetics is that you can get most of them wet without losing all their insulating qualities. Synthetic insulations are not absorbent; down is. You can wring out synthetics and they retain much of their insulating properties. Down, when wet, does not insulate.

But the tradeoffs remain. Synthetic insulations weigh more, cannot be stuffed into such a small bag, and they do not last as long as down when down is treated properly. Repeated use and washings tend to wear out synthetics.

Cost is another factor. While the initial investment in down is greater, it

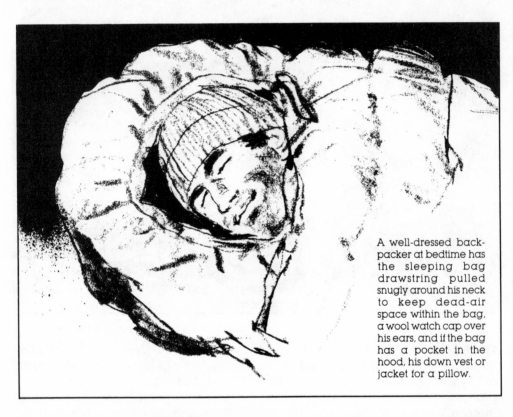

A well-dressed backpacker at bedtime has the sleeping bag drawstring pulled snugly around his neck to keep dead-air space within the bag, a wool watch cap over his ears, and if the bag has a pocket in the hood, his down vest or jacket for a pillow.

The basic shapes of sleeping bags are, from left, the rectangular, the modified rectangular, a modified mummy, and a pure mummy bag. Most backpackers use the mummy shape because of weight and insulation factors.

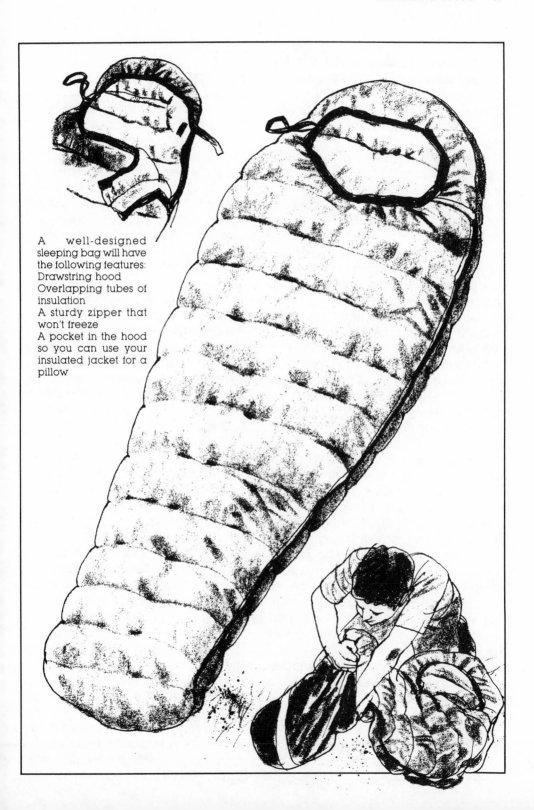

A well-designed sleeping bag will have the following features:
Drawstring hood
Overlapping tubes of insulation
A sturdy zipper that won't freeze
A pocket in the hood so you can use your insulated jacket for a pillow

is sufficiently durable to last literally for decades. Synthetics lose their loft over a period of time, making it necessary for you to invest in three or four new synthetic bags during your outdoor career.

Sleeping bags have been improved so much that outdoorsmen of the 1920s and 1930s would not believe the difference. Anyone who ever carried an old-fashioned bedroll of two or three blankets covered with canvas can tell you that not only were the bedrolls heavy, but they simply didn't keep you warm. Nor were they very comfortable to sleep in.

The modern sleeping bag is almost a joy, and some backpackers consider going to bed at night one of the joys of the sport. Parents have been known to hide sleeping bags from the children because nothing is quite as cozy as a sleeping bag with all its loft intact and its incredibly smooth liner of nylon.

Bags come in a variety of shapes—the two basic ones being mummy and rectangular. Mummy bags are the most practical for backpacking because they are lighter in weight for the same comfort range and they require less space in tents and stuff bags. Rectangular bags have the advantage of being more versatile. They can be unzipped fully and turned into a comforter at home, and two can be zipped together to sleep two adults or a covey of young 'uns.

In addition to these basic shapes, there are a number of modified shapes—the barrel, which is a bigger mummy; the tapered rectangular, which tapers toward the feet and a few other modifications that increase the size of mummies and reduce that of rectangulars.

THE INSULATIONS

With the advent of reliable synthetics for insulation in sleeping bags and clothing, a great deal of confusion has resulted. Obviously, no insulation is perfect, either natural or synthetic; and, as indicated earlier, each involves a tradeoff in weight, bulk, expense, and longevity. New products are being tested constantly and introduced on the market as the search continues for improvements in all factors.

Following is a primer on the insulations available at this writing. These are applicable to sleeping bags and garments. Only one synthetic, Thinsulate, is not commonly used in sleeping bags because . . . when compared to the soft fluffiness of its contemporaries . . . Thinsulate is too thin and somewhat stiff.

Down: This is the best insulation in the world and is the underplumage of geese and ducks closest to the underbody. A down cluster differs from a feather in that down does not have a shaft. Instead, it has a quill point around which a network of arms cluster and radiate outward like the tentacles of an octopus. The best down comes from birds that live in the coldest climates where the birds' bodies respond to the cold by creating more and better down to survive.

The best down of them all is from the eider duck, but don't expect to find eiderdown garments over the counter. Eiderdown is so limited and laws governing harvesting from wild duck nests are so stringent that it is no longer a factor in the insulation industry. However, as a point of information, the down comes from eider ducks and is picked from nests by hand. It differs from goose down primarily in its shape. Eiderdown has microscopic Velcro-like hooks that keep the down clustered together. Should you throw a handful into the air, it would cling together in a fluffy, almost weightless ball. Throw a handful of goose or duck down into the air and it will become a cloud.

Goose down is a crop. It comes from cold-country geese raised to maturity five or six months before the holiday season when a roast goose rounds out the festive year-end celebrations.

Duck down is also a crop but unlike geese that are raised to maturity, ducks are slaughtered for table fare at six to eight weeks of age. Duck down, then, is predominantly immature and weak.

Because down is such desirable insulation, and its supply limited, attempts by disreputable merchants to dilute their product led to the setting of rigid rules by the Federal Trade Commission.

BACKPACKER'S TIP

Spare clevis pins make good tabs for zippers on your parka or sleeping bags. Then you'll always know where they are when you need pack repairs.

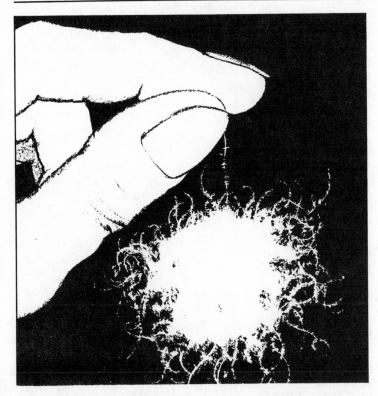

A cluster of goose down, magnified slightly.

In order for a product to be labeled "down," it must by law contain at least 70 percent down clusters and plumules (a downy, undeveloped feather with a soft, flaccid quill). This is the minimum requirement. The maximum percentages of other materials include: no more than 10 percent down fiber (detached pieces of clusters and plumules), no more than 18 percent waterfowl feathers, and a maximum of 2 percent residue.

Still another measure of quality down is its filling power. In this measure, an ounce of top quality down will fill 550 cubic inches of space in a special test cylinder.

How do you know you're getting down that meets these rigid standards? The safest way is to buy from a company that has a good reputation in the field, as well as a record of standing behind its guarantee. Pay attention to the "law label," which shows the content. Only a label that states "down" or "duck down" or "goose down" with no other embellishments meets the above criteria. Labels stating "80/20" down or that refer to any blend of down and feathers are something less.

As noted earlier, synthetic insulations have more than earned their place of respect in the industry. The first generation of polyester fill that was heavy and refused to compress has been improved dramatically in the past two decades. Here a few of the more popular insulations:

Quallofil: This is a new DuPont product made of short polyester fibers that have four microscopic air shafts in each fiber to trap air and create "dead-air" space, as well as the dead air between individual fibers.

Hollofil II: Also a DuPont prod-

CARING FOR DOWN GARMENTS AND BAGS

If you take proper care of your goose-down insulated clothing and sleeping bags, the down will easily outlive the fabrics that enclose it. The down can be used again and again in clothing and sleeping bags or comforters for decades. In order for them to last this long, they must be cleaned as needed and cleaned properly.

The first rule, an obvious one some people overlook, is to read the label that is sewn onto all quality clothing. In most cases, the instructions say to either dry clean or wash.

For dry cleaning, it is essential to find an establishment that has experience in dry cleaning goose down. It is best to ask a local outdoor-equipment store for recommendations (if you live near an Eddie Bauer store, they always keep a list of qualified dry cleaners).

The two most popular dry-cleaning solvents for goose down are Stoddard's Fluid and Perchlorethylene (Perk). Either is recommended.

It is best not to attempt to use coin-operated cleaning machines to clean goose down, in part because you can never be certain if the proper solvent is being used, nor can you be certain the dryers operate within safe heat levels.

If you decide to hand wash

your clothing and bedding, use a mild, bleach-free soap. Do the washing in a large sink, or preferably in a bathtub, using lukewarm water with only enough soap to produce suds. Gently but thoroughly work the suds into the garment or bag, **avoiding squeezing the wet down**.

In the case of sleeping bags, it will take about 12 hours to thoroughly clean a bag in a bathtub.

Drain the tub and rinse the garment thoroughly, gently squeezing the water in and out. Do not wring it.

Continue through several rinses until you are certain all the soap has been rinsed out. Any soap left in can cause the down to become lumpy.

If the garment is excessively soiled, you may have to repeat the process again.

If you decide to machine wash the garment, the large front-loading models found in commercial laundromats are the best. Use a mild, bleach-free soap and set the washing cycle to "gentle"; use only lukewarm water.

To dry the garment, gently squeeze—remember, do not wring—the garment to remove as much water as possible. Then carefully remove the garment from the tub or washer by lifting it from beneath without placing stress on the material or seams. It will be heavy; a bag can weigh 100 pounds. Place it in a large tumble drier. Set at low heat, add

a clean tennis shoe to tumble with the garment and distribute the down evenly as it dries and fluffs.

If time and weather permit, you can place your garment outside to dry in the sun. But be certain most of the water is gone to avoid damaging the fabric and interior baffles, and if possible, lay the bag flat on a picnic table or deck.

It will take from 6 to 24 hours for a sleeping bag to dry thoroughly in a clothes drier and at least twice that long when lying outside.

To store down-filled clothing and sleeping bags, do not leave them in stuff bags, because it destroys the thermal efficiency. Eventually the down will begin breaking down and the stress on fabric will be too great.

Instead, when you return from trips, remove bags and clothing from their stuff bags and let them air out for a few hours. Then store them flat or only loosely rolled up in a dry place.

Do not hang down-filled equipment on wire hangers or from clothes hangers if you can avoid it; but if you must, do not use wire hangers. Use broad wooden or plastic hangers.

All down products should be taken outside at least once a year to be aired.

When using down-filled products, always "shake well before using" to get the maximum loft.

uct that has been on the market for several years. Each polyester fiber has a single hole through the center for the dead-air space, and the fibers are treated to reduce friction between the fibers, thus making the insulation more supple and easier to stuff into a bag and fluff out again.

PolarGuard: A Celanese product, also made of polyester and cut from batts that are treated with resin to give them greater stability. PolarGuard fibers are continuous, unlike the Quallofil and Hollofil II fibers, which are cut to short lengths.

Thinsulate: This product is not used in sleeping bags, but is finding a growing market in clothing. It is considered too thin and the warmer batt weights are too stiff for use in sleeping bags at this writing. Its manufacturer, 3M, claims it insulates on a "boundary air" theory: a matrix of microscopic fibers traps air in and also holds molecules of air on the surface of the fibers. Thus, says 3M, it requires less loft to insulate than normal down and other synthetics. Thinsulate is made of 65 percent olefin and 35 percent polyester fibers.

TEMPERATURE RATINGS

All sleeping bags are rated within a given latitude of warmth, or comfort range. Those designed for summer use only may be rated down to freezing, or perhaps only 40° F. At the other end of the scale are the winter bags that are rated anywhere from freezing down to −20° F or even lower.

Clearly, no one bag can keep you comfortable in the Arizona desert and the Arctic mountains. As noted in the chapter on ultralight equipment, you have several options in making your bags more adaptable, such as adding a liner, a cover, or adding a so-called bivvy-bag and sleeping with your down clothing on.

The higher quality bags have both two-way zippers and Velcro fasteners along the zipper so you can partially unzip the bag on hot nights for ventilation. The better bags also have drawstring closures around the shoulders and head so you can make minute adjustments throughout the night, letting more or less air escape from inside.

A variety of construction methods are used in making bags, and these are important not only for their insulation factors but also for the bag's lifespan. Some of the key methods are:

Sewn-through: Stitches are run through both the interior and exterior of the bags to create tubes or channels to contain the insulation. This is common for lightweight bags designed for mild climates. It is of less value in cold weather bags because each seam is, in effect, a cold spot at the sewn-through juncture.

Slant box: Interior walls are sewn on a slant to form baffles that overlap and cover all seams with insulation to prevent cold spots. The higher quality bags use a fabric to accommodate the stretching and flexing of the body. Slant box construction also helps keep the insulation distributed evenly.

Slant box and Sewn-through construction are most often used for down insulation. The following are common with synthetic insulations:

Double offset quilt: The seams of two quilted layers of insulation are offset to maintain even lofting and to prevent cold spots. Common in warm-weather bags.

Sandwich method: An inner layer of insulation is sandwiched between two quilted layers of insulation and at-tached to the bag at the edges to prevent shifting. Primarily for cold-weather bags.

Other factors involving quality construction of bags include:

Stitching: Eight to ten stitches per inch is recommended. Fewer may loosen or snag easily, or let insulation "bleed" between compartments. More stitches may cut or weaken the fabric.

Differential cut: This is essential in all bags because the outer shell is tailored larger than the inner shell to permit full lofting and allow you to flex your knees and elbows without creating cold spots.

Side block baffle: A baffle inserted opposite the zippered side to keep insulation from shifting from the top to the bottom. This is used most commonly in down bags.

Baffled foot section: A baffle placed across the end of the bag to maintain even loft. Also used in down bags, usually in mummy-style.

Differential loft: Sixty percent, or a similar amount, of the insulation is on the top, where the body weight does not compress it. This gives better heat retention and does not waste insulation that will be compacted beneath you anyway.

Visible features you should watch for include:

Sturdy closures: Look for durable zippers, snaps, Velcro fasteners, and drawcords that operate smoothly. These closures are subject to stress, so be certain they work properly.

Two-way zippers: These are preferable because they allow easy and variable ventilation control. Plastic zippers (usually a type of nylon) are preferable to metal because they do not freeze as easily, do not conduct heat or cold, and are much less likely

METHODS OF DOWN CONSTRUCTION

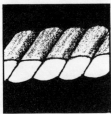

Sewn-through

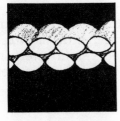

Slant-wall

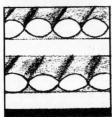

Offset quilt

Double offset

to rip the fabric should they snag. The larger the zipper the better.

SHELL FABRICS

Very few sleeping bags used by backpackers are made of anything other than nylon today. Cotton has been replaced because of its extra weight and its tendency to cling to your body when you turn.

The two major kinds of nylon used are taffeta and ripstop, both of which have great strength for their weight.

Taffeta is a softer fabric and excellent for the inner shell because of that softness and because it is rather slippery, which lets you turn in your sleep without turning the whole bag with you.

Ripstop nylon has extra heavy threads sewn through at intervals to stop rips and tears from spreading. Thus, it is popular for the outer shell.

PADS

The development of thin, lightweight pads that give you insulation between your body and the ground is one of the more welcome additions to the backpacking equipment list. Before they were developed, it was a challenge to find something—clothing, boughs, anything—that would insulate you against the cold from the ground.

Now we have the closed-cell foam pads that are an integral part of every backpacking trip. They insulate so well against the cold that it is now possible to sleep on frozen ground—or even a glacier—and be comfortable.

These foam pads can be rolled separately or wrapped around the sleeping bag while on the trail, giving some protection against snagging on brush and boulders. The pads can also be used as a seat when sitting on the ground or snow while having lunch or dinner.

Another alternative is the nylon-covered pads of polyurethane foam with washable covers.

All pads come in a variety of thicknesses, ranging from 1/3 to 2 inches. Unless you plan on some really cold-

BACKPACKER'S TIP

For an excellent substitute for the usual thin clevis pins, consider using spring-steel keyrings. They'll last longer and will not be so likely to snag on brush or material.

weather hiking, the thinner pads are usually sufficient and also lighter and more flexible.

AIR MATTRESSES

Very few backpackers use air mattresses because of the weight and bulk, plus their propensity for letting cold air slip in below you and convect

up into your sleeping bag. But newer models are now available that are self-inflating and are filled with a plastic foam that is similar to synthetic insulations. These mattresses are inflated simply by opening the valve that lets air rush in as the foam springs upward to open the cells. They are covered with waterproofed nylon that is also airtight. When your body heats the air trapped inside the foam cells, it forms a heat barrier between your body and the ground. Then the mattress is deflated by opening the valve again and rolling it up to force the air out. When rolled and with the valve closed to prevent air from rushing in, the mattress makes a reasonably small and light bundle, similar to that of a closed-cell foam pad.

CHAPTER 6

CLOTHING

Man is the only creature that cannot survive far from the equator without clothing. Why this is so is a subject for biological historians to ponder, but all seem to agree that it was necessity, not modesty, that led man to develop clothing. Even along the equatorial belt, clothing is often essential, especially in the deserts and shadeless plains, and even during tropical storms when the chill factor dips dramatically.

Until the last three or four decades—before the revolution in synthetic materials—the choices of clothing for backpacking were by comparison rather simple. We had choices of various woolen clothing, plus cotton and silk. For rain protection we had rubberized cotton. For insulation

we had kapok, down, and feathers, plus layers of wool.

These materials obviously worked well—and still do. But the overriding concerns have always been weight and thermal efficiency. As the population of the world increased and became increasingly mobile, and sports such as backpacking became more popular, alternate materials and insulations became necessary.

The plastics industry, an offshoot of the petroleum industry, came into its own during and immediately following World War II. As nylon replaced silk for parachutes, and then clothing, research and development on the nature and use of synthetics has not slacked off since.

For backpackers this has meant an

enormous range of materials from which to choose, and it appears that the state of the art in synthetic fibers and insulations may never be reached. New products are introduced nearly every year, and most offer improvements over earlier types.

However, as with all equipment where you have a choice between man-made and natural materials, there is always some form of tradeoff involved in the selection. No one material is an across-the-board substitute for another; each will always have certain differences that can be interpreted into advantages or disadvantages by the consumer. Obviously, you should know something about materials before making purchases of clothing and equipment.

UNDERWEAR

Personal preference plays a major role in selection of underwear, but the one item that is worn by most backpackers and other outdoors people the year around is the fish-net weave underwear. This does not provide warmth itself, but it does insure proper ventilation because it creates a very thin dead-air space between your skin and the next layer of clothing that helps wick your perspiration away from your skin while keeping that important insulating dead-air space next to your skin.

This is that all-important first layer of clothing, the real foundation in the

A classic example of the layering system is shown in this sequence, beginning with the hiker wearing shorts and tee-shirt. Then as the weather turns wet or chilly, he dons a pair of pants and an insulated vest, the latter to keep the trunk warm. Next, at night or higher elevations where the temperature drops, he changes to thermal underwear with the tops tucked into his woolen socks. The next layer is a parka and hat, followed by a rain suit and pack cover, and finally a poncho that covers the pack and the hiker. These are not necessarily in the order that each hiker would add layers, but they show the wide variety of layers of clothing to consider for various types of weather.

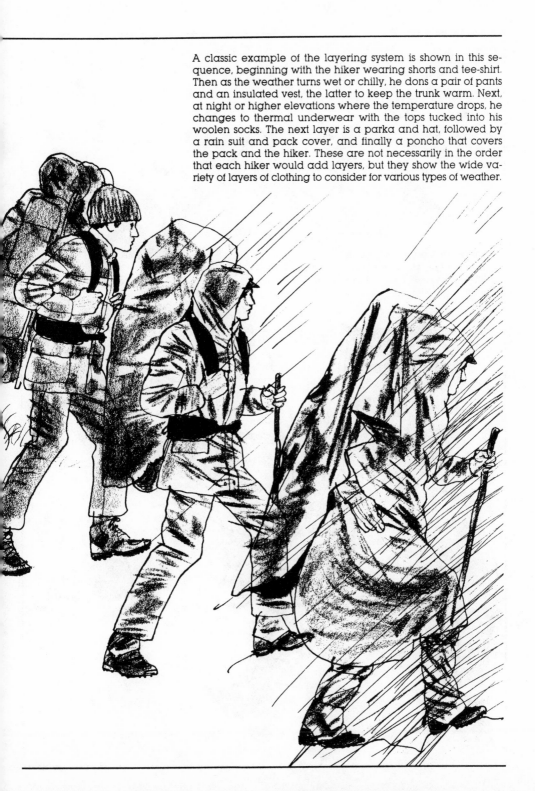

Shorts, long pants, and knickers with gaiters are common clothing for hikers of both sexes.

layering system, the only method of dressing for the outdoors that works for everyone.

The fish-net underwear is also important for the next layer of underwear for cold weather because it provides some protection against the itchy wool of some long-john underwear that you will want to wear during fall-to-spring outings. This second layer of underwear increases the insulation and enhances the dead-air space created by the fish-net.

PANTS AND HIKING SHORTS

Hiking shorts are popular in the more temperate zones of North America (but you should have a pair of long pants with you at all times as a backup in case of a sudden storm and the cold wind that it brings). These shorts can be of any material of your choosing, although cotton or corduroy are the most popular because they do not tend to cling or bind.

Your long pants should be made of wool or a wool blend for warmth and water repellence. Some specialists in outdoor survival are fond of saying that "cotton kills" because it has virtually no insulation qualities when wet. This may be a bit of an overstatement, but it is well worth remembering.

In addition to the insulation factor of wool and wool blend pants, it is important that they fit comfortably and do not chafe your legs or crotch. A place on your legs rubbed raw by too-tight pants is almost as uncomfortable as a blister on your heel.

Knickers are also popular be-cause the legs won't catch on brush, and they help with the ventilating process.

SHIRTS

What you wear over your torso depends on several factors, including your own metabolism. Some people have a higher metabolism rate than others and are warm even in a downpour; others are chilly while sitting on a hot rock in the blaze of noon. So you will have to make your own adaptations.

Generally, you can be quite comfortable in cotton tee-shirts and short-sleeved shirts during the warm day-time, backed up with a warm turtle-neck sweater and a long-sleeved wool shirt. Two tee-shirts and two short-sleeved shirts, plus the sweater and long-sleeved shirt will be sufficient for several days of hiking because you can always wash one tee-shirt and short-sleeved shirt each evening and let it dry while hanging from your pack the next day, if it doesn't dry overnight. Of course, many simply carry one tee-shirt and one short-sleeved or other combinations. You can make this decision after one or two trips.

Still another alternative for this shirt layer is to take along a goose down vest, which weighs no more than a wool shirt and can be stuffed into a package that takes less space than a sweater. You can wear it the first thing in the morning zipped up against the chill, then unzip it as the morning wears on and the temperature rises. And in the cool evening, a wool shirt over it gives you a very warm and comfortable layered system.

To repeat, a good, loose fit of shirts

is important for your comfort. Shirts and tee-shirts can be worn either tucked in or outside your pants.

PARKAS AND WINDSHELLS

The usual outer layer of clothing is the parka or wind shell, both of which are water repellent (**not** waterproof). Parkas come in a variety of materials, thicknesses, and lining material. They are made of outer material that is tightly woven, yet breathes so that you aren't wrapped in a material that keeps all the perspiration in. It is essential that this layer not keep moisture inside; if it did so, all your other clothing would soon be soaked. At the least, this is uncomfortable; at the worst, a cause of hypothermia.

You have a wide choice of materials from which to choose, but most are blends of cotton and nylon. A few are made entirely of nylon, but most have the cotton content to act as a moisture wick since nylon does not offer this advantage. Cotton will accept moisture, nylon will not. Also, nylon tends to be "noisy" when hiking through brush and is slick to the touch. Cotton softens both the feel of the material and adds a slight clinging quality to it, and it deadens the noise of rubbing the parka or shell against tree branches and brush.

You can buy parkas for nearly every temperature range, from desert heat to high-elevation chill. Some of the cooler designs are made of a tough nylon-cotton blend with a sheer, silky nylon liner to keep them from binding against your shirts and sweaters. As their warmth value increases, you have the choice of wool-lined parkas and on up to goose down-filled models. Some of these warmer models have zip-out linings to make them more adaptable for year-around use.

Sheer nylon wind parkas, or jackets, are popular for some backpackers who prefer wearing wool shirts and sweaters, or down vests and shirts. In essence, a wind shell then becomes the water-repellent last layer for your down-insulated undergarments. Another advantage to them is that since they are so sheer and lightweight, they

EDDIE BAUER ON SAVING MONEY ON CLOTHING

"Experienced outdoorsmen know exactly what will be needed for a planned outing and what may be required to cope with an emergency situation. These knowledgeable and seasoned people invest wisely in good equipment and avoid buying things that get stored away in closets to gather dust.

"The inexperienced have a tendency to be overly enthusiastic and seem to invest in whatever takes their fancy.

"To the inexperienced, I suggest . . . invest as little as possible and buy only bare necessities for short outings under favorable weather conditions. In this way, you build experience. Better yet, try to join experienced people on an outing or two. Soon you will learn about equipment and how to start investing in useful items that will give you a lifetime of service."

The range of insulated outerwear includes, top, vest filled with down or synthetic insulation; right, insulated parka; and bottom, uninsulated mountain parka.

often can be stuffed into their own pockets, then inserted into your shirt pocket in a package hardly larger than a wallet.

Both parkas and wind shells are usually made of ripstop nylon, or a similar product that does not snag or tear easily.

GLOVES AND MITTENS

It is always a good idea to carry a pair of gloves with a tough material over the palm, such as the work gloves with cloth backs and elasticized cuffs. They're useful for cooking, for handling rope, some repairs, and, of course, for keeping your hands warm during cold spells.

For cold-weather backpacking, or in northern climates where the temperature can vary widely on the same day, mittens are best for everything except chores where your fingers are needed. The best are shells made of leather or a tough synthetic with wool liners. Two pairs of liners should be carried so one can be drying while the other pair is in use.

Mittens are best for cold weather because you can rub your fingers together, make a fist, and conserve heat inside the shell. Gloves tend to isolate each finger from the other and keep them from sharing and conserving heat.

A poncho enables you to sit on a log or rock with your pack attached to your shoulders and still keep you dry.

RAIN GEAR

The last article of clothing for your torso is rain gear. Unless you are hiking in a desert where the last rainstorm occurred a decade ago, you should always carry raingear. The newer types are much more compact and lightweight than the old rubberized cotton, and often serve uses other than keeping you dry.

Each backpacker has a particular favorite. Some prefer pants and jackets; others swear by ponchos. Both have almost equal advantages and disadvantages.

Separate rain pants and jackets can be adapted to wind pants and jackets when a cold wind comes up unexpectedly, or at night around camp when your body is cooling off after a strenuous day.

But the disadvantage of them is that ventilation is difficult to achieve because they fit so closely to your body. If you are walking in a warm rain, eventually your perspiration will soak your clothing almost as much as the rain itself.

Ponchos have their loyal followers, mainly for the ventilation advantages. They can drape down over your pack, keep everything from your head to your knees dry, and still ventilate away your body moisture. They can be cinched at the waist to keep the cold wind away from your torso, or left to flap below the knees with air circulating all the way up to your neck.

And ponchos can be used as windbreaks, as canopies over the cooking area, and as groundcloths beneath tents or your sleeping bag. In a pinch they can be used as a tent by stringing a cord between two trees or sticks. You can sit on them during a lunch break to keep your pants dry. In the desert, they can be used as the plastic for a solar still.

Pants and jackets aren't quite so adaptable, but they have the advantages of being less likely to snag on branches and brush, and in a high wind won't act like a sail and flap in the breeze. The pants will keep your legs dry. Some have elastic cords that can be snapped around the bottom of your boot to hold them down over the boot tops to keep your ankles dry.

A few rain jackets are equipped with mesh screens beneath the armpits to increase ventilation while retaining the waterproof characteristics.

The most popular material of all for rain gear is Gore-Tex because it is both rainproof and breathable. This fabric is actually a membrane with an incredible nine million holes per square inch. Each pore is 700 times larger than a water vapor molecule, but several thousand times smaller than a drop of liquid water. So vapor escapes, but rain does not enter. Gore-Tex membrane is sandwiched between two sheets of breathable fabric for strength, durability, and ease of handling. Thus, it serves both as a good wind shell while still being waterproof. This material is the closest available to being the perfect choice for a parka and pants that double as wind and rain gear.

GAITERS

If you are hiking in snow or in a climate with frequent rain and heavy dew, you'll find gaiters one of the best accessories to insure dry feet and legs—

GAITERS

Styles of gaiters, from top, short, long zipped, long buttoned with Velcro adjusters, and homemade from plastic and string.

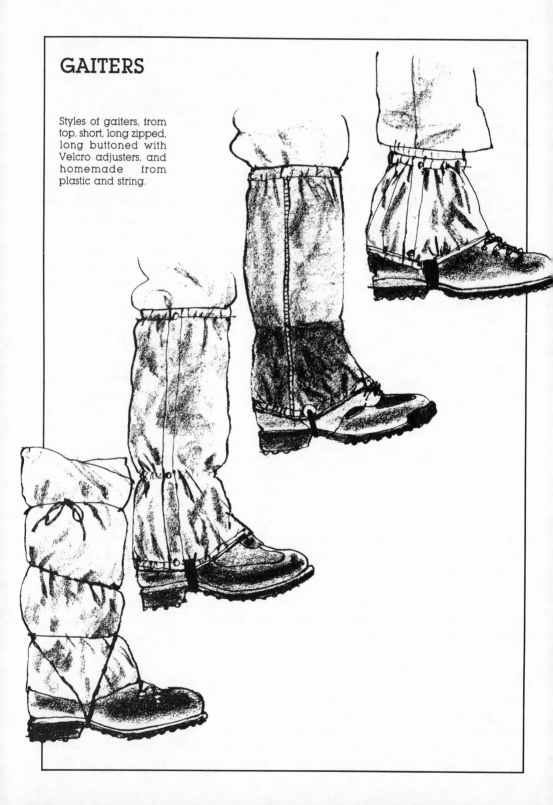

and **warm** feet and legs. You can find
them constructed in a variety of methods, from the old-fashioned laced leg-
gings to the more modern styles with
elasticized drawstring tops and zippers for ease of putting on and taking
off. Some have ingenious methods of
keeping them down over your boot
tops, such as hooks and eyelets to attach to your boots.

They are indispensable for keeping your legs dry when it isn't wet
enough to wear rain pants or chaps,
but too wet for simply wearing pants
and boots.

HEADGEAR

You'll find a wide variety of headgear
that is sufficient for hiking, including, from
top, watch caps, billed caps with ear flaps,
terry cloth crushable hats, and wide-
brimmed cowboy hats.

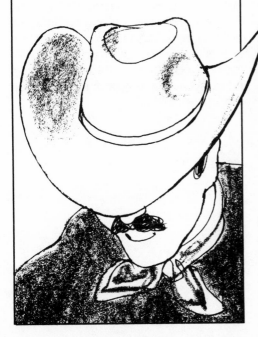

HEAD GEAR

The importance of a hat or cap is often overlooked by backpackers. It should be remembered that a large percentage of body heat is lost through the scalp and neck, where the blood vessels are closest to the surface. Thus, the old adage that if you want to keep your feet warm, wear a warm hat.

A wool watch cap is the most popular and most adaptable for warm-weather backpacking, because it can be worn as a simple cap covering the scalp only, or it can be pulled down over the ears and tucked beneath the parka or raingear hood. Or the hood can be brought up over the cap for increased insulation and protection.

When wearing a cap beneath raingear, many backpackers prefer a billed cap, because it keeps the hood away from your eyes and helps keep both sun and rain off your face. Another advantage to the baseball-style cap is that, unlike brimmed hats, the bill doesn't interfere with your pack, doesn't catch on branches so easily, and can be folded and tucked into a pocket or pack easily. Brimmed hats often have a tendency to catch on your packframe and be flipped off, although many backpackers are loyal

BACKPACKING CLOTHING LIST

Boots
Socks: Wool, outer; silk or polypropylene, inner
Waterproof gaiters
Underwear
Pants, shorts
Wool shirt or Chamois cloth shirt
Insulated jacket or parka
Insulated shirt or vest
Wind and rain parka
Rain pants, chaps, or poncho
Hat
Gloves

to their cowboy and Australian bush hats.

Another popular hat for backpacking is the terrycloth crushable hat that can be turned down to cover the ears and neck while still letting air circulate through. The material permits you to use the cap as a towel, as a pot holder, and a cooler simply by dipping it into a stream, wringing out most of the water and putting it on. The brim is less likely to catch on the packframe, and it can be folded or simply wadded into a lump not much larger than a bar of soap.

CHAPTER 7

FOOTWEAR

It is almost a tossup whether packs or footwear are the most important classification for backpackers. You can't go backpacking without both. And since both are so basic, many attempts have been made to reach the state of the art in boot design and materials.

Boots have gone through several evolutionary steps during the past few decades. Improvements have been made all along, especially recently with the advent of lightweight boots that also provide a firm grip on the terrain and warmth equal to that of heavier designs.

A good pair of boots can cost almost as much as a good backpack, and it isn't unusual for more than half the recreational budget to go for these two items. Since boots are so essential, you should shop for them as carefully as you do any major purchase. The pain caused by ill-fitting shoes is especially excruciating; and if you are miles from relief, your backpacking trip is a disaster. So shop carefully.

With no feeble pun intended, your hiking wardrobe and equipment list must have a stable foundation. Your boots support your weight as you scramble over rocks, ford streams, and undertake other activities your town walking shoes are never subjected to, plus your boots also support the additional weight you carry on your back. Thus, you need good, sturdy soles with enough arch support to keep your feet from getting tired or being injured.

Some backpackers wear only running shoes or tennis shoes and swear by them. Unless these shoes are quite well-built, meaning expensive, they aren't the best investment to make because they usually don't give the arch support needed and they wear out soon—with no opportunity to replace the soles.

Newer designs of hiking boots are substantially lighter than the kind backpackers have taken for granted for years. These new shoes weigh one to three pounds, wear like iron horseshoes, and keep the feet warm below zero. They still have the rigid soles for arch support, but instead of thick, stiff and heavy leather, they have synthetic material (such as Gore-Tex) and use plastic foam for insulation, similar to that used in ski boots. Some designed for summer use only are built on the same principle as basketball or running shoes, but with the required firm and cleated soles.

The cleated soles brings up another point on hiking boots: they are rough on turf, and they present a major problem on trails, meadows and campsites, because they are designed to dig into the soil.

Not too many years ago one of the popular slogans for wilderness preservation was "Take only photographs, leave only footprints behind." But with the boom in backpacking, these footprints became almost as much a problem as using packhorses in wilderness areas. A group of four backpackers can virtually demolish a campsite with the waffle-stompers, and a popular trail can soon become a ditch from being chewed up by backpackers trudging along day after day. In a recent effort to preserve trails and fragile meadows, the National Park Service began experimenting with outfitting their rangers in tennis shoes when they were out on day patrol only. And the word is slowly being passed along to backpackers to take along a pair of tennis shoes or running shoes to wear whenever possible. The idea is catching on, especially around camp where changing shoes is a welcome relief, anyway.

This isn't an easily solved problem, because the cleated waffle-stompers are almost essential for safety and certainly for durability. It is a problem to keep in mind when backpacking, and one that will only get worse.

One New England hiker researched the subject and found that one cleated-sole footprint left approximately an ounce of soil exposed and subject to erosion by rain. He carried the computations further and found that one hiker traveling one mile left 120 pounds of raised soil behind him. A party of four hikers with cleated soles would expose up to a ton of soil for every five miles they hiked.

This may or may not be an accurate estimation, but it does illustrate the problems these soles cause.

Other types of soles are available, and some backpackers simply don't like the cleated soles. Instead, they prefer the softer crepe-rubber or plastic substitute which have low ridges, or ripples and a steel-shank arch support.

There are other alternatives, and you can expect boot and shoe manufacturers to devote more and more energy and public relations money to this problem.

The matter of boot height is something each backpacker must decide for him or herself. Some like the lace boots that come halfway up the shin because of the ankle support they give.

The new generation of hiking boots is sturdy, waterproof, and breathable—thanks to Gore-Tex—and of equal importance, they weigh only a fraction of the older generation of all-leather boots.

Others are happy with the lower-cut boots that come to the ankle and stop. It is largely a matter of personal preference.

The important thing is that they fit properly. This cannot be overstressed. Unfortunately, only you can tell when a boot or shoe fits properly, because each of us has different preferences in fitting, and different feet function differently. For example, some feet tend to spread out—to splay or flatten with the addition of 50 to 70 pounds on them—while other feet change very little.

BACKPACKER'S TIP

It's always a good idea to carry a small amount of boot sealer along if you're on an extended trip. Used plastic film cans are good for this and usually hold enough for one treatment.

Some of us have high arches, others flat feet. So you will have to let your experience with other shoes, and especially work boots or hiking boots, tell you what to look for when you go shopping.

Generally speaking, you should have boots that fit snugly on the sides with a bit of extra space at the toe. But who can tell what snug means to each person? Not too tight and not too loose? That's as good a description as any. You will know when it feels just right.

Most backpackers wear two pairs of socks, a thin pair of cotton or silk against the skin and wool over those; so when you go boot shopping, be sure you take along the socks you normally wear with boots.

When you think you have a pair that will work, walk around in them, stamp your feet, kick your foot out in front of you against the floor as though you are descending a hill. If the store doesn't keep a pack around that is loaded with 50 to 70 pounds, take your own in with you and walk around the store for a few minutes, concentrating entirely on your feet.

Obviously the boots will need breaking in before they conform to the shape of your foot, but you are investing a considerable piece of your recreational budget and you must make certain the boots fit properly.

Don't be put off if the boots that fit you best are not the same size as the past pair you bought. Feet tend to flatten with continued use, and there is frequently variation within sizes anyway. Console yourself with the knowledge that American (and probably Canadian and European) feet are gradually getting bigger. Who cares?

Read the manufacturer's recommended methods of caring for the boots, and buy the cleaner or oil recommended. Always put them away clean and dry and on shoe-trees when you return from a trip. A good pair of boots will last for years with the proper care, another of those one-time purchases backpackers can make.

Except for some very lightweight and soft boots, the breaking-in process is a slow one. Plan on at least a week of fairly frequent use to mold the boot to the shape of your foot and to loosen the leather until it is reasonably pliable. Never stop by a store and pick up a new pair of boots on your way to a backpacking trip. That is courting disaster because discomfort and blisters are sure to result.

One of the best ways to break them

in is to wear them constantly after work; go for walks around the neighborhood and in the local park, applying moleskin to tender spots on your foot until the boots are as comfortable as any walking shoe you have owned.

Usually you won't have to apply oils or treatments to new boots, unless the manufacturer's recommendations call for it. Leather boots will have the natural oils in them. But after they are broken in and you head out on a hike, it is a good idea to apply one of the recommended treatments, such as mink oil or the silicone-based waterproofing salves, to protect the leather from water damage and to keep them from getting stiff at night.

Never, never dry boots in front of a fire, either a campfire or fireplace at home. Let them dry gradually and naturally. Speedy drying often stiffens them, at best, or damages them if they get too hot. If your boots become totally soaked from wading a stream or trudging through mud, wipe them clean and dry them as best you can with a cloth or rag, and then wrap them in something—a dirty shirt, for example—and keep them in the sleeping bag with you a night. This may or may not dry them out overnight (it probably won't), but it will at least keep them warm and pliable. Stuff a dirty sock or something absorbent in the boots at night to absorb some of the moisture.

If you are hiking in wet weather or along wet trails and are bothered by wet and cold feet, you can relieve some of the discomfort by inserting your stockinged foot into a plastic bag before putting the boots on. Few plastic bags will survive a long day of hiking, but it will help. In any case, it is a good idea to carry foot powder to help prevent the growth of odor-causing bacteria in your socks and boots.

SOCKS

Many backpackers devote a lot of attention to the proper selection of boots but give little thought to the socks they wear between the boots and their feet. Too many backpackers take a bit of discomfort for granted when it could be avoided by experimenting with the kind of socks they wear.

EDDIE BAUER ON FOOTWEAR

"In their eagerness to make a sale, some manufacturers go overboard by saying their boots are so perfect you can just slip them on and conquer Mount Everest that same afternoon. Well, that's simply not true. You just might sit in camp with wall-to-wall blisters while the rest of your party is enjoying the hike.

"Any footwear should be worn and worn, before you leave home, until it's fully broken-in. Jog . . . hike . . . cut the lawn . . . play golf in them; old shoe comfort comes only by working at it, but it sure pays dividends in the field."

The best combination of socks is a lightweight inner sock with a heavy wool outer sock. The inner sock should reduce friction by fitting well.

The best way to guarantee this is to buy sized inner socks, not the stretchable kind that fit a variety of sizes. Stretch socks often restrict blood circulation. The inner socks should be tightly knit, because you don't want anything coarse or rough against the foot. And the inner sock should also promote a positive wicking action to keep the foot dry.

Silk or polypropylene are ideal materials for inner socks when teamed with a wool outer sock. A highly absorbent wool outer will draw moisture out of the inner sock, leaving the foot dry.

Conversely, a wool liner combined with a synthetic outer will produce the opposite effect.

The outer sock should be a high-quality heavy sock with a high wool content—85 percent or more. The thickness of this sock is dependent on how much room you have in your boot. Go as heavy as you can but remember that you're better off wearing medium-weight socks than having your feet cramped and circulation restricted by too-heavy socks.

Tube socks are worn by many backpackers, but they have a tendency to bunch up around your toes and heel, since they have no heel construction to fit to your foot. Thus, they are not recommended.

If you feel either or both pairs of socks slipping down into your boot, stop immediately and pull them back up. To suffer along is almost a guarantee of a blister or at least a very raw spot—and in a very short time. To backpack with a sore hand or a stiff neck is discomfort; to backpack with a sore foot is agony.

If possible, change socks—both pairs—every day and let the others hang out to dry. Socks should be washed or at least rinsed out after every use, not only for the olfactory value

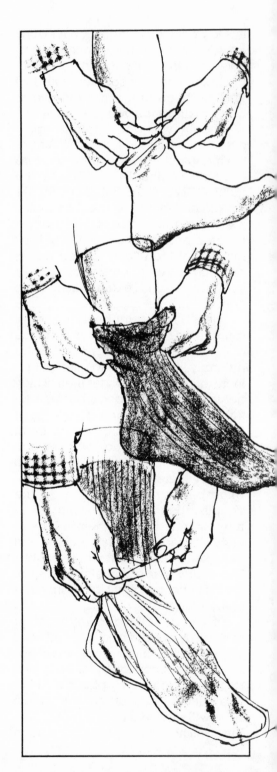

among your companions, but also because clean socks are more comfortable and give better insulation. A few grains of sand or dirt in a sock can cause a blister. A common sight on all trails is two or three pairs of socks flapping from backpacks as they hang to dry for tomorrow's use.

Some backpackers with leathery feet and ankles are not bothered by having wool socks directly against their skin, but most people get a severe case of the "scratchies" from direct contact, even those wool-nylon blends, which is another reason for the two-sock combination.

CHAPTER 8

TENTS

Tents for backpacking are frequently misunderstood by beginning hikers, because they expect more from tents than they're designed to give. Consequently, it is best to tell you at the outset what they do and do not provide.

They give you protection from the sun, but they are not air-conditioned. They will be hot on a hot day, but the sun won't be hitting you.

They protect you from the rain.

They protect you from the wind.

But they do not provide warmth and are not designed to hold heat. Instead, they are intentionally designed to be porous so that moisture will be carried off and away from the tent rather than collecting on the walls.

The rainfly keeps the rain off the porous inner wall, keeps the sun off the inner wall, and keeps the sharp wind from blowing through. Thus, while the tent does not provide warmth directly, it does protect you from the wind-chill factor. If you are in the mountains with the temperature at freezing or below and the wind is blowing, the actual temperature so far as your body is concerned is much lower. This is the wind-chill factor. But if you are inside the tent the wind-chill factor is **not** a factor in your comfort. By being out of the wind, you've eliminated that problem.

Backpacking tents have undergone many, many improvements in recent years. They have become much more sturdy while becoming dramatically lighter in weight. This light-

Dome tent

weight development in tents (and packs and boots, for that matter) is the most important factor in backpacking outfitting since freeze-dried and dehydrated foods.

At the same time, backpacking tents have become much more attractive than in the past. Colors are more vivid; and if you don't think warm, pleasant colors are important to one's mental well-being, try spending several days in an old Boy Scout khaki pup tent while your companions are in a brightly colored dome or wedge tent nearby. Colors and light on a dreary or stormy day do indeed make a difference.

These new designs are not only pleasing to the eye, they are also more efficient. The curved shapes are usu-

Tents are available in an almost bewildering variety of shapes and sizes. However, these three illustrations show the most popular types. The dome was one of the first departures from the standard A-frame pup tent design, and all models are freestanding. The ultralight tents are little more than a tube surrounding you and your sleeping bag, while the umbrella tent is the other extreme in spaciousness. These umbrella tents can hold three or more people, and by sharing the load—one person carrying the tent, another the fly and poles—it is manageable for many backpacking trips.

Ultralight tent

Umbrella tent

ally easier to erect, and they are better for windy and stormy conditions because they are more aerodynamically efficient. They are less likely to blow away like a paper bag because they do not act like a sail. The old-style pup tents and wall tents have that tendency.

For the backpacker on a trip of several days' duration, the overriding factor, however, is weight savings. Two- to three-man tents have gone down in weight from the first generation of lightweights from 12 to 15 pounds to only a third as heavy. And in the process they have become much more compact.

A new tent on the market is made of Gore-Tex, saving the weight and bulk of rain flies.

The tradeoff in all of this, however, is that the lightweights do require more careful treatment. You must be much more careful where you place them so that sharp objects don't punch holes in the sheer, waterproof bottom. They are much more susceptible to snagging and wearing at points of stress, such as pole sleeves.

This doesn't mean they're not rugged and can't be trusted under adverse conditions; but it does mean that they can't be treated as casually as a cast-iron skillet.

SHAPES AND SIZES

Although some models are large enough for a medium-sized person to stand erect, more and more tents are actually little more than tubes into which you crawl for sleeping or to escape the sun, wind, and rain while in camp. They have been pared down to the minimum requirements for people more interested in traveling than sitting in camp.

The basic tent still has the features associated with the first generation of backpacking tents. These include:

Waterproof floor: Nearly all tents have a floor of nylon treated with a waterproofing that also covers the first two or more inches of wall.

Insect netting: This is in addition to the door flaps that are either zipped or tied closed so you can sleep with the flap open and keep out insects. It also creates cross-ventilation for warm nights and to keep moisture levels down.

Breathable fabric: This is necessary to keep moisture from your breath and body from collecting on sidewalls and the top. In cold weather this moisture turns into ice.

Waterproof rainfly: This is essential since the breathable tent walls are porous. The fly is attached so that it is at least two inches away from the roof to permit air to circulate and blow away the moisture. The flies are also required to keep the sun from hitting the walls, which can be damaged by the ultraviolet rays. Some materials are not strongly affected by the sun, but most are. Polyester is an example of this, but it is more expensive than nylon products.

To a large extent, shape as much as size dictates the weight of tents. The larger they are, obviously the more they weigh. But enough backpackers who like space in their tents remain on the trails to keep the variety of designs broad. Although there is a tendency for people to follow each new concept in any sport without asking

Above: Rectangular shape sleeps four
Below: Geodesic backpacker sleeps three

themselves if the new model is really what they need, still there are those who would not part with their aging teepee-design tent or the old-fashioned but durable A-frame. To them, the additional weight is of less consequence than giving up something so familiar and comfortable.

The first real breakthrough in design was the elimination of interior poles, which had an irritating habit of collapsing and were always in the way. Designers came up with the exterior frame designs and saved a lot of tempers in the process. This design enabled those who love the old A-frames and pup tents to stick with their favorites.

Then came the dome tents, copied largely from Buckminster Fuller's geodesic design. These are some of the most visually pleasing designs in existence, and will always be favorites. This is in spite of the limited floor space in the three-person models, which due to their round floor requires two of the three persons to be rather short so their heads won't touch the walls.

A modified dome is an alternative development; it is actually a rounded A-frame that gives more head room than the straight, flat walls of the standard A-frame.

The latest generation of tents is the tube or tunnel designs that are similar to Quonset huts in that their walls form almost perfect half circles. Of course, these have undergone several variations, such as having the front higher than the rear, where your feet will be, and most now require fewer poles than earlier and the weight is thus reduced.

It should also be mentioned that part of this development resulted in the disappearance of external lines running from the peak and walls of tents for support. These lines, a bane to night walkers and forgetful or awkward campers in the daylight, became superfluous when the dome tents appeared because the poles, or wands, were passed through the sleeves on the outside of tents. Their tension not only kept the tent walls taut, they also made the tents self-supporting. It wasn't even necessary to use stakes, although they are recommended to keep your tent from blowing away in the first breeze that comes up.

TENT CARE

At the campsite: Sharp objects are the bane of backpacking tents, so carefully examine the ground before you pitch the tent to be sure all stones, protruding roots, and twigs are removed before the tent is erected. The best protection is a groundcloth, a waterproof tarp, or section of plastic sheeting placed between the tent and the ground both to protect the floor and to keep the tent dry.

Nearly all backpacking tents are made of material that will weaken after repeated exposure to ultraviolet rays from the sun. But the rainfly is not susceptible to these rays, so always put the fly over the tent.

Storage: You should always make certain your tent is both clean and dry before putting it away after trips. Wet tents can mildew, which not only weakens the fabric but also creates unpleasant odors. Dirt and sand left inside the tent act as an abrasive and wear away at the fabric. So when you return home from a backpacking trip,

Put up your tent in the backyard before each back-packing trip to be sure all the parts are still there and that no repairs are needed. This also airs it out, removing unpleasant odors that might collect. At the campsite, as soon as everyone is up and out of the tent, it is a good idea to turn it on its side (if it is a self-supporting model as shown here) or take it down and lay it bottom-side up to dry the condensation that collected during the night.

erect the tent on the lawn, patio, or in the family room and thoroughly clean it. After sweeping or vacuuming out the dirt, wipe the tent clean with a solution of water and baking soda, allow it to dry thoroughly, and store it in a cool, dry place in its stuff bag. Be sure the stuff bag is clean, also.

Do not store it in the car trunk or other hot place for any length of time because high temperatures can also weaken the fabric.

Leaks: Buy seam sealer, available at nearly all outfitters, and use as directed, even on new tents, because the majority of leaks occur in the seams. Check seams frequently for signs of extreme wear and apply the sealer as needed.

Cleaning: All quality tents come with the manufacturer's recommendations for cleaning compounds that are safe to use. A mild solution of water and baking soda is the most common. Many, perhaps most, cleaning compounds can damage tents, especially those of petroleum derivatives.

Staking: More and more tents are self-supporting and do not come with lines that must be staked. However, always take along aluminum or hard-baked plastic stakes and use them as anchors to keep the tent from blowing away.

Poles: Keep the poles and fiberglass wands clean and free of corrosion. If a burr develops on metal poles or connectors on fiberglass wands, buff it down with a fine sandpaper or nail file. Not only will the poles and connectors work better, they will not snag on the fabric if they are kept smooth.

Shock cords: If your tent does not have shock cords as part of the original equipment, it is a good idea to install them, especially in lieu of the grommets commonly used around the floor to hold the tent against the ground. Shock cords are elasticized cords that are available in small loops or in lines. They will help relieve the stress on tent fabric caused by wind and shifting bodies inside. They are also useful in anchoring the rainfly, which is more susceptible to stress from the wind than the tent itself.

Shock cords are also very useful in assembling hollow poles. By running a shock cord through aluminum poles, all it takes to assemble them is a snap of the wrist. Also, the cords keep all components together so that fumbling around for a complete set of poles is eliminated.

Zippers: The best zippers for tents are large plastic ones rather than metal because metal zippers freeze easily and also corrode. Metal slides on plastic zippers work well, however. Plastic zippers should be lubricated frequently with light silicone, which comes in either stick or liquid form. Unless you are going on an extended backpacking trip, an application before each outing is usually sufficient.

Chemicals: Be very careful of letting chemicals, such as hair spray, be used near your tent. Most stove fuels can also damage tent fabric.

Familiarity: Be certain you know your tent well and can erect it even in the dark. Examine floor models before you buy, and have the salesperson show you how to erect it before leaving the store. Then practice erecting it a few times at home. Many backpackers have less than fond memories of trying to erect a tent in the darkness with the wind blowing and the rain falling. Nearly all tents have their peculiarities and their little tricks that ease the erection process.

Tarps serve a multitude of functions, and one of the most important is as a wind- or rainscreen over your cooking area. A tarp strung between two trees and anchored firmly will offer a surprising amount of protection.

Fire safety: Most tents manufactured today (except Gore-Tex) are treated with chemicals to render them fire-resistant. This does not mean they won't burn, only that they won't turn into a torch. Check the specifications before buying because most, but not all, states require that tents be treated with a flame retardant.

Some tents designed for expedition and winter use have zippered cookholes in the center of the floor so you can place the stove on the ground instead of the waterproof bottom. Use these only when absolutely necessary because your tent can be badly damaged by spilled food and fuel, and the danger of burning holes in the floor is always present. Consequently, fewer and fewer tents offer cookholes now. As an aside, these zippered cookholes are virtually impossible to keep waterproof, even with liberal coatings of seam sealer. If your tent has one, you should plan on always having a ground cloth beneath.

TARPS FOR SHELTERS

A few die-hard backpackers still insist the only shelter you will need for fair-weather backpacking is an eight-by-ten foot waterproof tarp. Under the best of conditions, you can get along very well with a tarp that is either supported by a line between two trees or poles or made into a lean-to with only one support line from a tree branch above.

But for most backpackers, this is living a bit too close to the elements because it assumes you won't be caught in a rainstorm that inevitably whips rain inside a tent that is open on one or both ends.

Tarp shelters are also obviously an open invitation to insects that can fly or walk right in to feast on your exposed face and hands.

Still, there are those who prefer traveling as simply as possible and who feel cluttered with technology when they are confined to a tent at night. The choice is yours.

BACKPACKER'S TIP

Some backpackers add extra protection to their tent floors by placing the closed-cell sleeping pads beneath the floor. They accomplish the same insulation while also keeping sharp objects away from the tent fabric.

CHAPTER 9

ACCESSORIES

One way to surprise yourself—if not frighten away beginning back-packers—is to load your pack with everything you will need for a week's outing, then unload it and lay out everything on the living room floor or deck. You will be surprised at how many individual items you are carrying in your pack and equally surprised at how lightweight and compact everything is.

The temptation is always to carry that something extra that you "might need" on a trip. Many backpackers carry one or more of these items, never using them but feeling more secure with them around. This does not include the Ten Essentials. It can be a Swiss Army knife with fourteen blades when three will be sufficient. Or it can be a miniature chess set when nobody else in the group knows or cares how to play the game.

However, you should have a small repair kit that you may never open. But when repairs are needed, you'll bless yourself for taking it along. The kit should include a pair of pliers—an indispensable tool for most repairs, as well as for use around the camp for a variety of tasks. You should have spare D or O rings to replace those on your pack, a needle and thread with either sturdy nylon thread or a roll of dental floss for repairing tents, packs, and even boots. You can also carry some spare grommets, although the best for emergency use is the ball-and-wire variety that can be used anywhere on a tent or tarp that you can gather a small amount of material together.

Another item you should always

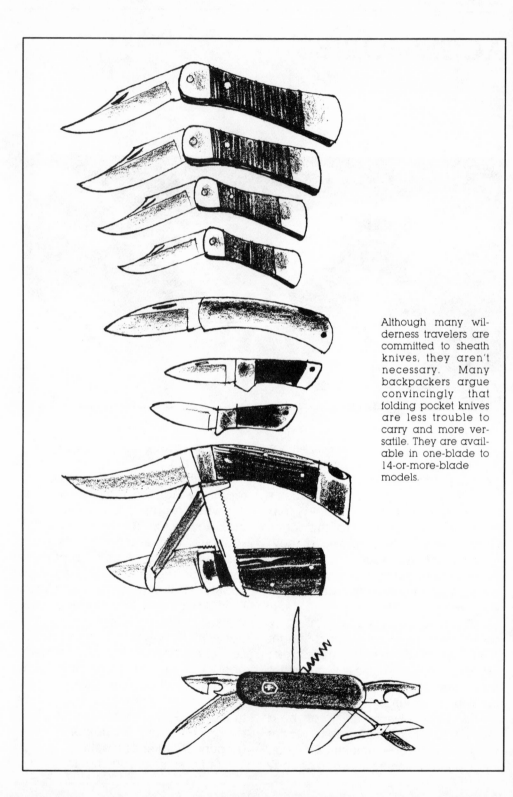

Although many wilderness travelers are committed to sheath knives, they aren't necessary. Many backpackers argue convincingly that folding pocket knives are less trouble to carry and more versatile. They are available in one-blade to 14-or-more-blade models.

carry, or someone in your group should have along, is about 60 feet of at least one-fourth-inch nylon climbing rope. This will almost always be used, either for such mundane campground uses as stringing a clothesline or tarp sunshade, to such emergency uses as building a litter for carrying out the injured. Nylon rope is fairly light and incredibly strong.

If your weight allowance permits it, you should also consider carrying binoculars. They have practical uses, such as searching for routes across snowfields and spotting companions some distance away. And they are convenient for nature studies, such as

EDDIE BAUER ON ADDING LIFE TO RUBBER-COMPONENT SPORTING GOODS

"Air mattresses, rubber boots and waders, inflatable boats and so on, should be kept away from oil, grease, gasoline, and petroleum products . . . all of which rot rubber. Sunshine, too, hastens the destruction of rubber. Hang your rubber waders by the feet uncreased. Cracks develop when rubber is folded."

BACKPACKER'S TIP

A pair of ordinary pliers is one of the best tools you can carry with you on a backpacking trip. Their uses are as wide as your imagination permits. They are excellent pot holders, can be used for innumerable chores around the cooking area, can be used to untie stubborn knots, or to tighten lines that may cut into your hands, and for almost all repairs to tents, stoves, and other equipment. Sharpen one handle and you have a screwdriver. And you can scratch that spot on your back your fingers can't reach.

bird watching and observing various kinds of wildlife.

Most backpackers are also photographers. Some carry not one but two cameras, one for black-and-white photos and the other for color. Unless you are marketing photographs, one camera with a zoom lens, and perhaps a micro or macro attachment for closeups, is usually sufficient. And you can always have your choice color slides made into black-and-white photos or into color prints.

While you will definitely need a knife, you do not need a Jim Bowie Special that hangs almost to your knee and catches on brush as you stalk along the trail. In most cases, a three- or four-bladed pocketknife is sufficient. A modified Swiss Army knife with two or three blades plus a screwdriver and a can opener on one of the blades is about all you'll ever need.

If you carry a sheath knife, you'll almost never have a need for a blade more than three inches long. Be sure it fits snugly in the sheath. Some are equipped with rawhide or plastic thongs that help hold the knife in.

THINGS YOU DON'T NEED

A folding foxhole shovel, circa World War II
A nine-pound hammer to drive tent stakes
A crescent wrench
Camp stools and folding chairs
Cosmetics (or even deodorants)
Hatchet*
Saw*
Firearms*

*Recommended for primitive area trips and survival situations

CHAPTER 10

THE TEN ESSENTIALS

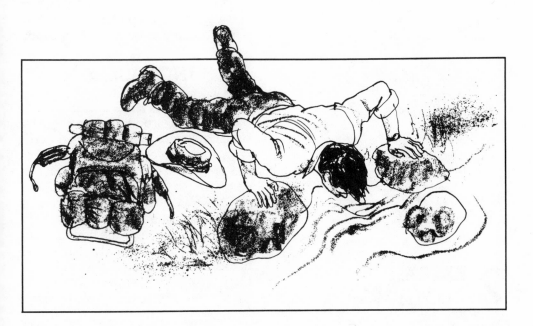

Few pieces of backpacking and camping equipment have received more attention—and deservedly so—than the so-called "Ten Essentials" for survival. Safety in the wilderness cannot be overemphasized. Although mankind originally was as much at home in the wilderness as the wild animals that live there today, most human instinctive survival skills have been forgotten over a period of many centuries. Only through very specialized training can anyone today hope to survive in the wilderness without these ten items.

Remember: our sense of direction and our ability to spot danger signs before the danger itself arrives are not nearly as acute as we prefer to think they are.

So take this list of the Ten Essentials very, very seriously. Consider these items as important to your backpacking trips as boots and food. Kits with these items are available and will be discussed after each item is explained.

1 SURVIVAL KITS

In meeting the demand to save space and weight, a number of quite ingenious survival kits have been developed—many packed in cans no larger than pipe-tobacco tins (in fact, many are packed in these tins) and weighing little more than a pack of playing cards. Yet these kits contain everything essential for surviving at least one night in the wilds, sometimes longer. A typical kit contains:

Tube tent made of dark nylon
Whistle
Candle
Matches
Duct tape
Aluminum foil
Energy candy bars
Bouillon cubes
Nylon cord
Signal mirror
First aid supplies
Fire-starter pellet(s)
Razor blade
Dextrose cubes
Herb tea bags
Waterproof survival data

2 EXTRA CLOTHING

You should always have warm and dry clothing in your pack in case a sudden storm blows in, or in case the clothing you're wearing gets soaked by a dunk in a stream or by simply traveling through wet brush. Also, you need extra clothing to dress by the layering system to keep you warm at night. Keep this extra set of clothing—a pair of wool socks, a wool shirt or turtleneck sweater, and pants—wrapped in your pack in a plastic bag.

3 FLASHLIGHT, SPARE BATTERIES, AND BULB

If you have a reading addict in your group who cannot consider sleep

without reading a few pages or chapters each night, be sure you have spare batteries and an extra bulb hidden away. A dead flashlight will not help you signal at night, nor will it help you find your way if you are only a few yards from the camp in a black night.

4 SUNGLASSES

This item, frequently ignored by backpackers, should always be carried. They are essential when camping in the open country of the desert or plains, as well as in all mountain areas where the presence of snow is a factor and where the sun bears down more directly without the benefit of air pollution to soften the rays. An elastic holder or strap should always be attached to keep them from falling off when they catch on brush or even when you lean over.

BACKPACKER'S TIP

A good way to waterproof your matches is to dip them in shellac, which is both easier and more efficient than wax.

---

5 EXTRA FOOD

Each person in your group should always have an extra day's supply of food, and it should not be touched except in emergency situations. Don't torment children (and most adults) by

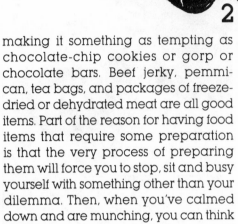

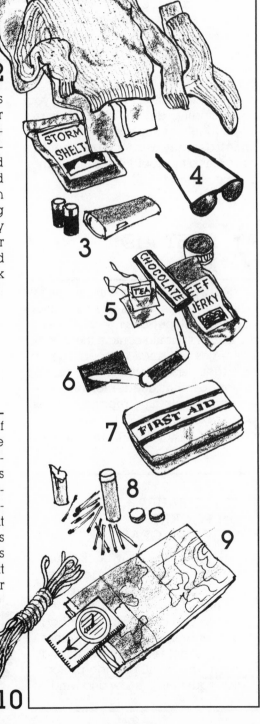

making it something as tempting as chocolate-chip cookies or gorp or chocolate bars. Beef jerky, pemmican, tea bags, and packages of freeze-dried or dehydrated meat are all good items. Part of the reason for having food items that require some preparation is that the very process of preparing them will force you to stop, sit and busy yourself with something other than your dilemma. Then, when you've calmed down and are munching, you can think more clearly.

6 KNIFE AND SHARPENING TOOL

Some backpackers, especially of the male gender, feel undressed in the wilderness without either a short bayonet hanging from their belt or a Swiss Army knife of such gigantic proportions that it has a dozen tools combined into one—and is so bulky that it wears holes in pockets and causes blisters or callouses on legs. There's nothing wrong with these knives that have all the attachments, but smaller ones similar to the old Boy Scout knives with the big blade, a can opener, an awl, and a screwdriver are sufficient. For a belt knife, one that is no longer than 8″ overall (and therefore has a short blade) is perfectly adequate. Also, it is less likely to get hung up in brush or to frighten little children when you come striding down the trail toward them. In any event, a sturdy knife has almost as many uses for a backpacker as a complete tool kit has for a mechanic.

7 FIRST AID KIT

No two first-aid kits will contain exactly the same items, due to differences in each person's needs. However, the basic kit should contain these items: Band-Aids for small cuts; gauze pads of various sizes; adhesive tape; salt tablets; aspirin; needle for blisters or emergency clothing repairs; a single-edge razor blade; Halazone tablets or similar method for purifying water

EDDIE BAUER ON POCKET SURVIVAL GEAR

"Include in your back country gear a couple of large plastic garbage bags. When you're pinned down by bad weather, cut the end of one garbage bag and wear it as a skirt. In the other bag, cut holes for your head and arms. These will provide protection against rain, snow and wind."

Headlamp with battery pack

Adjustable-beam flashlight

Techna 2000 high-intensity light

Waterproof lamp with waterproof batteries

FLASHLIGHTS

Carbide lamp

Twelve-volt lamp with separate battery pack

(new products are available to replace or complement purification tablets); first-aid cream; a mild antiseptic, such as Bactine ; antihistamine tablets for bee or hornet stings; and, where required, a snake-bite kit. And, of course, include any prescription drugs you must take regularly or in emergencies.

8 MATCHES IN A WATERPROOF CONTAINER

Small containers for matches are available in a variety of shapes, made from a variety of materials. The best are made of metal with a striking surface either on the outside of the container or inside the cap. Some backpackers glue a small piece of sandpaper inside the cap as a backup system, in which case the matches should be stored heads down away from the striking surface. Be sure you have the "strike-anywhere" kind of kitchen matches, and don't use them for anything other than emergencies. Carry them in your pocket at all times. A few stubs of household candles scattered throughout the backpacking equipment are always welcome for starting fires. And reserve one for emergencies only. A good solution to the problem of keeping them separate is to have an unused candle in your parka or pants pocket at all times (the "emergency candle"), while using the stubs for normal firestarting. However, since fewer and fewer backpacking routes permit campfires, your candles will be used only for light and emergency firestarting.

As an aside, many backpackers new to this form of recreation are not aware that candles are excellent firestarters. To use them, whittle up a good supply of shavings from a dead tree branch or other tinder, such as pine or spruce needles; then light a candle and drip wax liberally over the tinder. When you have a good coating of wax built up, place the candle beneath the pile of wax-coated tinder; shield it from the wind and light it. The wax will ignite—in turn igniting the tinder.

Chemical firestarter has become more popular than candles. This slow-burning chemical comes in either pellet form in waterproof cans or in a heavy liquid form packaged in plastic containers that are easily torn open. Both forms ignite readily, burn long, and are more reliable than candle wax. If you have a chemical firestarter, consider carrying a candle anyway, so you will have a source of light at night.

9 MAPS

These include road maps and topographical maps of the offroad areas in which you'll be traveling. If you are in a national forest or national park, these agencies have excellent maps that are a bit more manageable than the topographical maps. Store them in waterproof cases and be certain you know how to read them.

10 COMPASS

As with maps, know how to use one and be certain the maps you carry have the compass declination factors

printed on them. As explained else-where in this book, the declination is . essential for proper pathfinding.

And all this in a carrying case that fits in your parka pocket!

Another popular item that is found in many kits is the "space blanket," forerunner of the newer insulation called Thinsulate. These blankets are extremely lightweight and compact, yet they will reflect up to 80 percent

BACKPACKER'S TIP

Although the metal match container with a rough cover for striking matches is still the best solution to keeping matches dry, you can substitute this with a pill bottle that has the so-called "childproof cap." Glue a bit of sandpaper under the cap and you have a waterproof container that weighs less than a metal one.

of your body heat back onto you when you're wrapped head-to-toe in the blanket.

Admittedly, some of the items found in most survival kits have little to do with survival beyond giving you something to occupy your mind for a few minutes while you collect your thoughts. Thus, the tea bags have little or no nutritional value, but most peo-ple tend to calm down while building a fire, boiling water, then sipping a cup of tea. These few minutes of make-work are often the most important few minutes of being lost in the wilderness; it is during this time that you will make the important decision of whether to continue walking or to sit tight. Or you can spend those few minutes while you wait for your water to boil to look over your map or maps once again to try to locate yourself. If you can spot a dominant landmark, chances are you can find it on your topographical or Forest Service map; then by a process of triangulation, you can find out roughly where you are as you stand waiting for your cup of tea.

EDDIE BAUER ON WET WEATHER BACKPACKING

In the fall of 1914, when I was 15 years old, I was hiking in the hills on my way to some steelhead fly fishing in the Stilliguamish River northeast of Seattle. I'd just topped a rise when I heard rhythmic chanting that sounded like Unn! Unn!. I sat down and pretty soon I saw about 20 Indians hiking single file. Those in the rear were toting large bundles of supplies and had their hands full. Those at the head of the line . . . three sturdy young men in their teens . . . had a staff about 5 feet long in each hand. They used these staffs to reach ahead on the trail to shake the water off the ferns, conifers and shrubbery in their path. Pretty smart! This way, they shook the water onto the ground, rather than having it soak their clothing. On your next wet weather backpacking trip, take along a ski pole or two. You'll stay drier and climb hills easier.

PART III
ON THE
TRAIL

CHAPTER 11

ENJOYING THE HIKE

Since America has become so urbanized, many people grow to adulthood not knowing how to walk properly away from paved streets and paved walks in city parks. Thus, it is necessary to spend a few minutes considering the major differences between urban walking and backpacking.

First of all, you've probably never walked in the city with a load of 35 pounds—or perhaps as much as 60 pounds for a long trip—strapped to your back. You have always judged distances by blocks rather than by miles or kilometers. You are accustomed to having lots of people around to ask for directions should you lose your way or be in a strange city. If you slip and sprain an ankle, you are sel-

dom more than a five-minute taxi or ambulance ride for help. A phone booth is at the next corner.

So with this as your background, you now find yourself at a trailhead, the end of the road, with a pack to put on your back and a trail to follow that leads off into the wilderness.

The first mistake most beginning backpackers make (some never change, for that matter) is trying to walk as though nothing were on their back and they were simply walking up a steep sidewalk. Each person has a pace that is the most comfortable, and it may be faster or slower than that of others, your companions included. You should find your pace as soon as possible, because it can mean the difference between hiking tired all the time, or hiking with a great deal of ease while still covering several miles each day. Hiking too slowly can be almost as tiring for some people as trying to hike too fast. A steady pace with even strides and frequent pauses is the most efficient way to travel in the woods, and those frequent pauses can be only a minute or two to stop and lean against a boulder or tree trunk.

Now is the time to look behind you. Even though you are on a well-marked trail, you should always keep yourself oriented, even though you plan to return over the same trail. An occasional glance backwards will make your return trip easier because you'll know the trail better. Also, you will never get lost if you are among familiar landmarks.

No matter how many times you have backpacked, the first few yards are usually a period of adjustment. The pack and its straps will feel great when you first swing into the pack, but your pants belt may be in the wrong place, or the hipbelt of the pack may be too tight or too loose, and the shoulder straps invariably need adjusting. Or your pack may have to be reloaded with the weight more evenly distributed. So there is a host of fine-tuning adjustments to make when you're just starting.

After this is completed and you have hiked several minutes, you may be ready for a break to catch your breath. It is easiest to find a bank, a fallen log or stump, or a boulder to lean against with the pack's weight taken off your hips and shoulders. Sometimes you will be lucky enough to find a bank or boulder at exactly the right height so you can remove the pack completely without having to wrestle it back up to your knee, then

around your shoulders again. In this case, remove it and walk around a bit, swinging your arms and letting the perspiration dry on your back and shoulders where the straps and pack-frame rode against your body.

If you are traveling with companions—and you should rather than alone—everyone will probably have to make some minor personal adjustments to match the group pace. It is best to stick reasonably close together, not only for safety but also for companionship. The leader, who may charge ahead and spend a lot of time waiting for the others, will become as grouchy as the caboose hiker who straggles far behind and seems to catch up with the group only in time for them to announce it is time to leave again. So sticking together definitely promotes harmony in the group.

It is a good idea to have a modest supply of trail food in a convenient pocket—gorp (raisins and nuts) or high-energy fruit bars—and to take fairly frequent nibbles of them to keep your energy level high.

Don't try for too many miles each day. Trying to cover too much distance can quickly turn a leisurely backpacking trip into a marathon where the only thing you see is the trail ahead or your companions' boots. You can accomplish the same thing by running on the local public school's track.

After you have hiked a few times, you will have a good idea of how many miles you can go each day without pushing yourself and your companions unduly, or without getting bored walking at half your normal speed. You'll have to select hiking companions with similar interests in speed and distance.

Backpackers have their own forms of courtesy, which when followed do not interfere with anyone's enjoyment of being on the trail. Noise is frowned upon, because sound carries long distances in the outdoors, and it is unnecessary except in times of emergency. Seasoned backpackers get quite grouchy about noise; they have been known to steal batteries from portable radios and to build bar-

ricades to keep trailbikes off trails dedicated to foot traffic only.

When trails wind back and forth along the face of a hill, you should never cut across one of the switchbacks, because that only invites erosion that in one rainstorm can wipe out several feet of trail.

Always be aware of the person ahead and behind you. If you should accidentally dislodge a rock, tell your

Don't crowd on the trail; you're liable to step on your companion's heels, and you'll be so busy watching where you step that you won't see the scenery.

companions or other hikers immediately so they can dodge it. The same rule applies to traveling through brush. Don't let branches swing back and swat those behind you; either ease the branch back to its normal position, or give those behind you an opportunity to catch it and hold it out of the way.

Don't crowd the person ahead of you. Keep at least three paces behind, preferably more, so you will have a chance to dodge dislodged rocks and won't bump into the people ahead when they stop suddenly. Besides, it can be nerve-wracking to listen to footsteps directly behind you and to hear someone breathing virtually on your neck. Nearly everyone has a personal "space" requirement—that distance you like to keep from other

people. In the wilderness, that space grows larger with most people, so try to avoid "invading" others' space.

Always yield the right of way to faster hikers who are trying to pass you. When you are passing other hikers, give them plenty of warning—a simple "May I pass?" is sufficient.

Also yield the right of way to uphill travelers, because they are working harder than you are, and let horses and pack animals go past without delaying them. When they do go past you, make no sudden moves that might spook them. Frightening animals is not amusing to pack-string owners and is dangerous for all involved.

Plan your day's travel so you will have camp set up well before dark. You can do this in a variety of ways if

INTERNAL PLEASURES

Although we like to think that all backpacking trips, all routes, all countryside are fascinating every inch of the way, sometimes a particular route will be—well—boring. Some places are like that, especially open country you have to go across before reaching the timber and water again. The problem is how to put in a few hours of straightforward walking without succumbing to boredom.

Most of us have our antidotes to boredom. We mentally conduct Beethoven's Ninth (glowering at the soprano, who is too loud again!), or we try to remember the poetry of Longfellow or Dylan Thomas or the plot of a J. D. Salinger short story. Some people daydream, a rather old-fashioned term for what pop psychologists today call "fantasizing."

In other words, you have to draw on your own resources. And if you are the type who has to be amused and entertained and catered to by others in order to get through the day, you may find much of backpacking tedious. So know thyself before striking out on a long trek. You may save yourself—and certainly your companions—some irritating moments if you can keep your own counsel during the flat periods that occur in nearly every trip.

Not all backpacking moments can be grand and glorious and exciting. The ancient curse, sometimes credited to the Irish, other times to the Chinese, "may every day be interesting," applies to these trips. Backpacking can be all the wonderful things, and it can also be punctuated with nonevents: just walking.

you're traveling on an unfamiliar trail. Ask the park or forest ranger to mark potential campsites on your map that might not be shown there. You may have to cut one day's hiking short and make the next day a bit longer in order to have good campsites. It is far better to leave at the crack of dawn than to hike until the last ray of sunlight disappears. You must be able to see the trail for safety, so do not get caught by darkness.

Most maintained trails have footbridges across streams, but certainly not all. Also, bridges have a habit of being washed out by rainstorms or spring melt. When you come to a stream that must be waded, it is best to take off your pack and walk up and down the stream, if possible, searching for the shallowest and broadest portion. It is also best to avoid fallen logs across the streams (unless there are two together intentionally fallen by the agency that controls the land and with steps or notches in them). Most fallen logs are slippery, and it is better to get your feet wet than take a chance on slipping and falling and hurting yourself. Stepping stones in the water are usually slippery, too, so look for a gravel bed, small rocks, and shallow and slow water.

If none of these are possible, you

HOW TO CROSS A STREAM

The first thing you must do, no matter how tame the stream seems (the step-across varieties excepted), is to completely loosen your hipbelt and let all the weight ride on your shoulders. Too many backpackers have stories of slipping, falling into a stream, and "turning turtle" with the pack weighting them down while they wrestle with the hipbelt to escape. It may often be a source of campground hilarity later, but it is an experience of stark terror, grave danger, and great discomfort at the time it happens.

If the crossing is easy—shallow or slow water without great danger of slipping—simply re-

The illustration shows the proper way to ford an unfamiliar stream; boots off, hipbelt unfastened, and a sturdy stick for the tripod effect.

move your boots and socks, tie the boots together to drape around your neck, and walk across carefully.

A walking staff is always handy for stream crossings. Many backpackers feel under-equipped unless they have some kind of stick with them at all times. When you cross streams, staffs are very helpful in keeping your balance by finding a good purchase for them on the stream bottom, then stepping ahead. Put a bit of weight on them as you step, but not so much that you can topple over if the stick slips.

In faster water, you must exercise additional caution. Sometimes it is best to remove your boots, but leave your socks on, because they are more likely to find a good grip on slippery stones than your tender and smooth feet.

Also, when wading fast water, the best angle is slightly downstream rather than straight across, because as you place each foot forward, it is easier to swing it with the current until you find solid footing. Again, you are less likely to lose your balance if one foot is slightly downstream from the other. You can wade across at an upstream angle for the same reasons, but the downstream angle is best.

If the stream is really fast and dangerous, and you have no other choice but to cross in a swift current, it is often best to strip down to your underclothes and socks, tie one end of your rope to a boulder or tree (the latter preferably) and go across carefully, paying out the rope as you go, so that if you fall, you will have it to cling to. On the opposite side, tie the rope to another tree or boulder, or wrap it around them and hold it while your companions cross behind you, carrying their packs with hipbelts loose. This means, of course, you will have to go back to the other side for your own pack, and someone will also have to cross and untie the rope.

Some backpacking parties get quite clever with these stream crossings, using two ropes to make an aerial tramway; and some who know they will have rugged streams to cross carry a light-weight pulley or two with clothes-line-weight rope to build a cable system. But this is too complex for the average backpacker who wants only to cross a small stream without needing a background in civil engineering.

BACKPACKER'S TIP

It is a good idea when crossing streams to wear a pair of wool socks and carry your boots. Wool socks will help you grip slippery rocks and even provide a bit of protection from the cold water. Then wring them out and hang them on your pack to use to wear the next stream or to start drying.

Use a line for crossing deeper or swifter streams.

can protect yourself and your companions by taking off your boots and wading across with one end of a line tied to your waist and the other held by a companion on the bank. Do not try to stride across swift water. Instead, walk sideways, either facing the current or with your back to it. A walking staff is invaluable here because you can use it for a tripod effect, always having two points of pressure against the bottom.

When you reach the other side, tie the rope to a tree or boulder, or stay there and use yourself as the anchor, and have the others grasp it while fording the stream. It is best to hang your boots around your neck and walk across on wool socks because they provide some grip even on slippery stones. The last person across is tied to the rope for safety and uses a walking staff for further safety.

In the case of a sudden cloudburst that causes a stream to rise dramatically, it is far better to wait on high ground for the stream to subside than to try to force your way across. A stream swollen by a cloudburst will fall almost as quickly as it rose, and the wait is worth it.

Except for stream crossings, you should always try to remain dry while backpacking because excessive perspiring means excessive cooling when you stop or when a brisk wind comes up. Don't hesitate to stop to remove too-warm clothing; and by the same token, don't hesitate to stop to put on more clothing to stay warm. One of the most effective means of controlling the body temperature is to wear a hat when you are cool, then remove it when you become too hot. This is possible everywhere except the desert where you should always wear some kind of head protection.

BACKPACKER'S TIP

If you like hiking with an alpenstock or a favorite walking stick that doesn't have a good handgrip, try using bicycle handlebar grips made of rubber. You can heat them in hot water to stretch them so you can place them on the stick; then let them cool and shrink firmly on the stick.

DAY HIKES

Many backpackers become involved in the sport after a few family-camping trips where they set up camp in a government or private campground and then went on short day-hikes to see more of the countryside while getting some exercise. The usual way this evolves is first to purchase a small knapsack or rucksack to carry spare clothing, lunches, and the Ten Essentials. When they find that backpacking isn't so hard and that there's a lot more country to see, and in more pleasant situations than car-camp-grounds, they begin looking into larger packs, lighter clothing, bedding, and kitchen equipment.

True, some people jump straight into backpacking with all the proper gear on their back for the first trip, but for most it is an evolutionary process. In their desire to get away from the highways and roads, they may decide to carry their equipment in to a small lake or to a campsite they discovered on a previous trip that is less than a mile from the parking lot. But if you ever tried to carry a wall tent under one arm and a two-burner stove in the other hand, and then had to go back for food and a sleeping bag, you probably marked that date in your life as the day you decided "lightweight" and "compact" were words that applied to something other than automobiles and small prizefighters.

Still, day hikes are a reasonable way to find out if you really want to commit yourself to backpacking. Perhaps you find you enjoy day hikes enormously, but the thought of carrying all that weight, spending all that money on equipment, and sleeping away from the sound of a highway are all much too primitive for your taste. If this is the case, you can still enjoy hiking to the fullest simply by going on day hikes with a small knapsack and comfortable shoes or boots.

Don't be lulled into thinking that day hikes don't require the same safety precautions involved in backpacking. If you're on a five-mile hike and you become lost, or a storm blows in, or you injure yourself two miles from the trailhead, you had as well be 20 miles from the trailhead if you are not prepared.

The same rules ("safety precautions" is a more pleasant description

Winter camping requires additional specialized gear and is growing in popularity, partly because of the growth of cross-country skiing.

but "rules" sounds more official, so we will stick with the word) apply to both day hikes and wilderness treks, and they are based on the principle that anything bad that can happen eventually will happen. So be prepared.

Each person on a day hike should have the Ten Essentials, especially those relating to clothing and food. It is possible to pool some of the items, such as medical suppplies, but the party cannot be split up if these items are spread among two or more persons.

Thus, one of your first purchases should be a survival kit for each per-

son. Keep it sealed, so nobody will be tempted to take out the contents to look at them—or worse, to use some of them—without replacing them. Buy or create kits for each person, put their name on them, and seal them with sturdy tape.

Many hikers, particularly the youngsters, enjoy wearing as few clothes as comfort and community standards permit. There's nothing wrong with leaving on a hike wearing only shorts and tee-shirt and boots, but in your pack should be warm pants and shirt or jacket—and not cotton. Some survival experts strive to make

their point with cotton by stating, over and over at times, that "cotton kills." This can be true when hypothermia is a threat, but certainly not when heat is the problem. If your major danger on a day hike is the sun, then you should substitute a loose-fitting cotton shirt and pants for wool pants and shirt.

We will discuss hypothermia and heat stroke and prostration elsewhere in this book.

The terrain largely determines the kind of shoes or boots you need for day hikes. If you are hiking along well-used and reasonably level trails or across open and flat fields, ordinary walking or running shoes are sufficient. Your load won't be heavy, and your only other concerns will be crossing streams or encountering local problems, such as chiggers, ticks, or poisonous snakes. In each of these cases, you should wear long pants; they can be sprayed with insect repellant from the knees down to keep ticks and chiggers from hitchhiking onto you. If you hike in an area known to have poisonous snakes, you should wear boots that come at least up to your shins, although thousands of farmers, ranchers, and walkers in general avoid problems with snakes simply by watching where they step. Snakes won't chase you; on the contrary, they will attempt to get away from you. Only when they are cornered or surprised will they strike; and in spite of our common fear of snakes, extremely few people are bitten each year. And very, very few of those die.

The list of places to go on day hikes is limited only by your own imagination and interests. In nearly every major metropolitan area you can find large parks, and on the outskirts of the city there are game refuges, dike roads, river roads, old canals, and so forth.

Although walking has been popular in Europe, and particularly in England, for centuries, only in the past two or three decades have North Americans discovered how interesting it is to drive out into the country, park the car in a safe place, and walk along country roads.

For example, in the Pennsylvania Amish districts, you can take a step backward, technologically speaking, and walk through the farming area where you will see horses being used for power and transportation and never hear the sound of a motor. Or in the northern states of Minnesota, Wisconsin, and Michigan, you have a wide choice of country roads, some unpaved and hardly used, that let you enjoy the countryside and wildlife while still being within sight of farmhouses and small towns.

To repeat, only your imagination limits your day hikes. No matter where you live, you can buy county maps that show every road, every lane, and every small town. From these it is easy to select a circular route for a day-long hike that costs you nothing more than the gasoline to get there and

back. You can usually make arrangements with a farmer to park your car on his property, or leave it at a service station or even at the local sheriff's office or police station, while going for your day hike.

By scouting around rural areas, you will find a wide variety of places to spend an afternoon or weekend hiking. Many farmers and ranchers don't mind having hikers cross their property provided they are asked politely and are assured that all you intend to do is walk through their property. Many long-lasting friendships have been formed this way.

Obviously, when hunting season opens each fall, it is time to put away the walking shoes and knapsack and to find other pursuits within the city limits.

When you cross private property, always do everything in your power to create no problems for the owner. Be very careful climbing over fences to avoid damaging them. Check the posts to see if they are solidly implanted in the ground before you climb over a wire fence. If you have to cross barbed wire, you can usually do so by crawling through the strands. But take off your knapsack first and have your companions hold the wire apart, so you can get through safely.

In cattle country the ranchers often build steps over fences where frequent crossings are made. Always use these steps instead of stretching the wire or pulling out staples accidentally by stepping on the wire at the post.

Do not scare cattle. Walk past them slowly and quietly. This is especially important when walking near dairy cattle because excited dairy cows do not give as much milk.

If you see a bull, don't go near him.

Some bulls will charge you and some will not. You'll never know which one is the mean one until he breathes down your neck. The owner is never amused, either.

If you go through a gate, always be certain it is securely locked after you. This sounds so obvious that some readers may feel insulted, but it always amazes farmers and ranchers that people would use a gate without closing it. But they do, by the hundreds and perhaps thousands each year.

Other choices for day hikes, and certainly the most popular ones, are within the national forests and national parks where the scenery is more likely to be beautiful and wild. The headquarters personnel, particularly local rangers, are your best source for suggestions on day hikes. The days of free Forest Service maps are gone, probably forever, but the price ($1.00 each at this writing) is still very reasonable for the amount of information, the variety of trails and terrain shown, and just for the beauty of the maps. They are the next-best thing to topographical maps, and they have prettier colors.

LIVING WITH THE ANIMALS

The best way to approach the subject of dealing with wild animals in the wilderness is to treat them the way they treat us—stay away. But mankind has a greater fascination for other species than any other creature on earth. For some unknown reason, we are drawn to wild animals and cannot seem to leave them alone.

Of all the animals encountered in North America, the only one that attacks out of sheer meanness is the grizzly. Other creatures, including poisonous snakes, prefer to run and hide from man.

In dealing with bears—all species—give them the right of way at all times. While only the grizzlies are frequent attackers, other species, such as the common black bear, will attack under certain circumstances. This is particularly true when you find yourself between a sow and her cubs. As cute as cubs are in their awkward enthusiasm, they can mean only trouble if you get too close to them.

If you are backpacking in grizzly country, such as parts of Wyoming, Montana, Canada and Alaska, check with local rangers and law enforcement agencies before heading out on the trail. They can tell you of any recent sightings or trouble areas.

In any case, you should take as many preventive measures as possible. Although backpacking is essentially a silent sport, if you are in bear country, be sure the bears will have a chance to move on before your arrival. Make enough noise for them to know you are there. Some backpackers carry small bells on their packs as a warning. A metal cup that clanks against your metal packframe is another method. The noise doesn't have to be on the order of a portable stereo with a rock tape blaring. But make some kind of noise that sounds man-made.

In campsites, the best thing you can do to avoid bear problems is to hang your food from a tree branch at least ten feet high and several yards away from your camp. Do not create a garbage pit, and if you are in an established campground, avoid camping near the garbage area.

Skunks are another problem in the

Hang food out of reach of bears and other animals

EDDIE BAUER ON WILDLIFE PHOTOGRAPHY

"Travel quietly and speak softly. Constantly sample the direction of air flow. Expect to see animals upwind from you—never downwind—unless the animal is stalking you.

"All land animals fear man as a predator . . . a fear that dates back through evolution . . . instilled by the scent of man leading to and from kills.

"Animals have keen ears, eyes, and noses even when bedded down. They feel the vibrations of man's heavy footsteps at great distances and are able to slip away. This ability to feel man's presence undoubtedly led to the Sioux belief that deer possess six ears . . . two on the head and one on each hoof that sensed footsteps at a great distance."

woods because, with good reason, skunks aren't particularly easy to frighten. There's hardly a mature animal anywhere in North America that does not know what it means when a skunk turns its back and lifts its tail. The musk from skunks is one of the most overpowering and clinging odors in the world. If you are unfortunate enough to be sprayed by a skunk, you'll have little choice but to bury your clothing on the spot and take repeated baths. If your equipment is sprayed, you had as well plan on replacing it.

So it is wise to give them a wide berth. If one strolls into camp, let it do as it pleases. Usually it won't stay long when it realizes it is among people. Fortunately, it does not spray except in fear or anger. So if you leave it alone, it will usually go away.

Another camp visitor that can be a tough customer if you get too close is the porcupine. Most people have enough common sense to stay away from them, but pets do not. So if you have a dog on the trip with you, don't let it get near the porcupine. Few things cause more agony for a dog than those barbed quills that usually must be removed by a veterinarian. Unlike skunks, you can take measures to frighten porcupines away from camp. But you must be patient in driving them off because they are a bit dimwitted and slow. Frequently they crawl slowly up a handy tree and sit there looking as though they forgot how they got there.

A common mistake made by people everywhere upon finding a young fawn is to assume it has been either abandoned by its mother or that the mother has been killed. Wildlife managers have been trying to educate the

When a skunk
comes calling,
beware!

public on this for hundreds of years, still with only limited success. The truth in every case is that the doe has run away in an attempt to attract attention to herself instead of the fawn, but the person who finds the fawn didn't understand her signal. The doe will almost always be within sight, or at least scent, of her offspring and will return as soon as the invaders leave. There is no use in going some distance away from the fawn and watching because the doe will stay out of sight as long as you are nearby.

Never pick up a fawn and carry it away. Often the doe will then abandon the fawn, even if you put it down again. For this reason, it is against the law nearly everywhere to "adopt" fawns and other young animals.

To repeat, the best method of dealing with all wild creatures is the same way they deal with us—leave them alone and keep your distance. Try to avoid surprising them.

This applies to all snakes in North America as well. All kinds, poisonous and otherwise, first try to escape from us and attack only when cornered.

WILDERNESS HOUSEKEEPING

Only a few years ago the North American wilderness was so vast and so unexplored that the matters of pressing concern among wilderness managers today did not then exist. Anyone over 40 years of age can remember when it was safe to drink from any stream, when nobody cared about not leaving footprints behind because there were so few footprints that it didn't matter. They can remember when roaring campfires every night—and at lunch and breakfast—were perfectly acceptable wilderness behavior. Nobody thought it unwise to fell mature trees for wood and saplings for tent poles, and it was very common to cut a thick, fluffy bed of boughs for a mattress each night.

In those reasonably innocent days, garbage—including tin cans and bottles—was routinely buried rather than carried out. Living off the land (shooting game) was not only common, it was preached to novice outdoors people as a way of life.

Nobody suspected until just after World War II that the wilderness might one day be laced with an intricate network of trails; that every stream and lake would be in danger of becoming cesspools and garbage dumps. After all, when only one or two hikers

You should carry sturdy stuffbags for garbage and a general catch-all.

dumped their uneaten food into a lake each year, little damage would be done.

Those days of innocence are apparently gone forever. Even the most remote wildernesses, such as the Canadian and Alaskan Arctic, are routinely traversed by helicopter and kayak and on foot as backpackers range to the far reaches of land all over the world.

Consequently, at the continual risk of sounding like a concerned mother scolding a child, an educational process has been created and the teachings have been constantly repeated over the past few decades. Inroads into the old—and today irresponsible—ways of dealing with the wilderness are being made; but the message, as

basic as it may seem, must continually be repeated and enforced if the wilderness is to remain in a relatively "natural" state.

While it is true that mankind is, after all, simply another species that uses the land, much as a beaver or an elk that isn't particularly tidy with its sanitation habits around water, still we must remember that we outnumber each of the species using the wilderness and that because we use tools and manufacture equipment, we can be very destructive without realizing it. Thus, the continuing education program.

A number of basic recommendations—"rules" in most managed wilderness areas and many heavily used national forests and parks—

NATIONAL PARK SERVICE TECHNIQUES FOR MINIMUM IMPACT

The National Park Service gives these guidelines for minimum-impact camping:

- **Plan ahead**: Choose trips you are in condition to handle. Familiarize yourself with where you are going by studying maps and guidebooks.
- Limit your party size.
- Excessive noise, such as yelling or radios, and bright colors psychologically shrink the wilderness.
- Leave rocks and flowers where you find them so others can enjoy them, too.
- Campcraft (rock wind screens, wood construction, trench lines around tents, and so on) are unnecessary and destructive.
- Pets, dogs in particular, are a threat to wildlife and an aesthetic intrusion for other hikers. Do not feed wild animals. Feeding creates unnatural, unbalanced populations that become dependent on unnatural foods.
- Use a campstove instead of wood campfires.
- Pack out your litter, including leftover food.
- Latrines should be dug five or six inches deep (within the soil's biological disposer layer) at least 300 feet from water.
- Washing should be done at least 300 feet from water sources. Minimize your use of soap since even biodegradable types are pollutant.
- Stay on the trail. Do not cut across switchbacks.
- When hiking off-trail, spread out abreast rather than single-file.

should be remembered. Some of them are:

CAMPSITES

Use only existing campsites when at all possible. If you must camp on new ground, do not disturb the area and do not leave any evidence that you camped there. The next group through the area may see evidence of former campers and assume it is a designated campsite.

In all campsites, avoid environmental damage to the area. Do not break off twigs and branches of trees, and do not enlarge the campsite by clearing brush. Use the established fire ring and the original rocks that surround it rather than blacken new rocks.

If you must clean the fire ring (if, indeed, fires are even permitted and wood is there for that purpose) carefully spread the ashes over a wide area back in the woods.

Do not assume campfires will be permitted everywhere, and always be prepared by carrying packstoves and sufficient fuel for the entire trip.

When you are packed and ready to leave the campsite, check the area thoroughly not only for small articles that may have been left behind, but also for ways to erase your presence, such as smoothing the dirt, and by all means pick up all garbage and carry it out. You should carry a sturdy bag, preferably nylon, for removing garbage with you.

On the subject of fires, always find out first if they are permitted, and if so, always use down and dead wood only. Keep the fires small, do not leave them unattended and use only enough wood for cooking purposes. Be sure the fire is completely out by drenching the area in water and digging down a few inches and turning the soil upward to be certain a root isn't smouldering.

If you must use something other than tent poles to keep your tent standing, use a standing tree or a branch. This is virtually obsolete due to the construction of modern backpacking tents, but do not cut saplings for this use.

Do not dig trenches around your tent. This was a common and accepted practice for decades to keep your tent floor dry. However, most modern tents have a waterproof floor that comes up the tent wall a few inches, and a door flap that is high enough off the ground to keep water

LATRINES

"Cat" toilet

Trench latrine

from seeping in should you be caught in a downpour.

LATRINES

You should carry a small digging tool for latrines. It isn't necessary to carry a folding G.I. shovel for this purpose; a small metal or hard plastic digging tool available at most outdoor suppliers is sufficient.

Although some groups prefer digging a trench and filling it in after each use, most backpackers prefer digging individual holes six to eight inches deep. After use, they can be filled in and the sod, if any, replaced.

Latrines should be at least 200 feet from camp and the water supply.

In groups of mixed genders, it is common for the women to go one direction away from camp and men an-

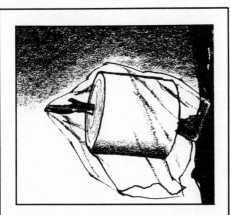

Protect toilet roll with a plastic bag.

other. If this isn't possible, an alternative is to have a roll of toilet paper suspended from a tree branch or some other obvious place. Thus, when someone goes to the latrine, no announcement is necessary. If the toilet paper is gone, the latrine is in use.

GARBAGE

Very little garbage will accumulate if you plan your food carefully. Avoid excess food by preparing only what you know you will eat, and do not carry food packed in metal cans if possible. Most backpacking food is packaged in either plastic or foil, both of which can be wadded into small and virtually weightless wads for ease of carrying out to the trailhead.

Do not bury garbage because it not only is unsanitary around campsites, it is also an invitation to wild animals to begin depending on campsites for food. This can lead to disaster in the case of bears, and irritation in the case of porcupines, skunks, and ground squirrels, the latter of which is soon an expert at robbing packs and food supplies.

In the case of dishwater and wastewater from sponge baths, do not pour the water in or near sources of fresh water, and do not pour it near the campsite to create a small swamp. It can be used to keep a campfire from spreading by pouring it in a ring around the boundary of the fire. It can also be used to douse a fire when breaking camp. Again, since so few wilderness areas permit campfires, this use of waste water is not really a factor any longer.

Waste water should be taken some

distance from the campsite, the trail, and sources of water. A good rule is at least 200 feet from all places just listed. Then dispose of it with a good toss rather than digging a little hole with it.

You should also be sure you are using biodegradable detergents because some detergents damage plantlife.

You shouldn't wash dishes in streams or lakes.

CHAPTER 12

DESERT TRAVEL

Most backpacking occurs in temperate to cold climates and in the higher elevations of the Southwest. There is an obvious reason for this: desert hiking is less comfortable and more potentially dangerous than hiking elsewhere. Water is scarce, heat is intense and in the cooler seasons or higher elevations, the nights are colder. Since the desert is so barren of vegetation and moisture, both of which are climate regulators, extremes in temperature are the rule rather than the exception.

Yet backpacking is not at all uncommon in the desert; thousands of people do it every year from West Texas to California and north into the High Oregon Desert. Colin Fletcher became one of America's most famous backpackers from his solo expeditions down the Grand Canyon and across Death Valley.

Backpacking in the desert—and enjoying it—requires particular attention to water, clothing and shelter. You cannot assume you'll cross streams as you might on mountain and Great

Plains backpacking trips. You must have enough with you when you leave to last until you return, plus enough for emergency use.

You must wear the proper protective clothing, and you must carry shelter appropriate for the desert heat, wind and even the occasional cloudburst. Of equal importance, you must know where to camp at night and during the heat of the day; how to avoid the floods that come sweeping down dry washes or arroyas; how to get the maximum shelter from the sun and the wind; and when to hike and when to hole up for the day or night. And, you must know the habits of rattlesnakes and other desert creatures which bite and sting.

First of all is water. Be sure your route will have water available on it, a year-around source, and if it is not

SOLAR STILLS

If you are hiking in the desert or plains where no water is readily available within a few hours' hike, you should carry a solar still with you at all times. They are simple to use, weigh only ounces, and occupy very little space. And they can save your life.

The still is composed of two basic components: a six' (or larger) square of clear or almost clear plastic and a container, preferably plastic. A cereal-sized bowl will work. A third component recommended by many desert travelers is a long (4' to

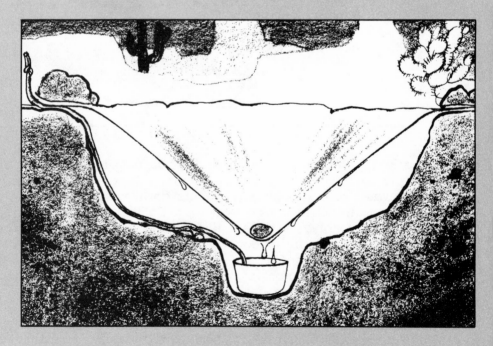

available, be prepared to carry a lot in your pack. The first generation of canteens made of metal, usually aluminum, are not recommended because such canteens are so easily punctured. The plastic models are best because they can take an enormous beating without showing a scratch, dent or puncture.

If your trek is going to be a long one, you should plan on caching water one day's hike out—more if it is a long trek. To do this, you and a companion carry a gallon or more of water each in a sturdy plastic container one day's hiking distance, bury it in the dirt or sand, and clearly mark its location so you'll recognize it when you arrive. Some extra-careful desert hikers have been known to take Polaroid photos of the cache to be absolutely certain. This procedure can be carried out for

6') piece of plastic tubing, the kind you see in home aquariums.

To use the still, dig a hole in the sand or dirt about 2' deep and 40" wide, tapered into a cone shape. Place the container in the center of the cavity. Then if you have the tubing, place one end in the container anchored with a stone or stick so it will stay in the bottom of the container, and run it back away from the cavity.

Then place the plastic over the cavity and anchor the edges with small stones or anything heavy. Push the center down so that it forms a cone, also. Place a small stone or other similar object in the center so that the cone of the sheet ends just above the container. The plastic should not touch the soil except at the rim. Cover the entire rim with dirt and sand to seal the hole as completely as possible.

The device works as a solar still. Heat from the sun passes through the plastic and heats the soil, causing water in the soil to evaporate and collect on the plastic. As droplets form, gravity forces them down to the bottom of the cone and they fall into the container.

The hotter the sun, the better the still works.

You can add vegetable matter to the bottom of the cavity, and if you are stranded in your car, you can pour your rusty radiator water (if it doesn't have antifreeze in it) down the hole. Urine can be used, since the evaporation process purifies it. In the latter cases—where you have water available—you should have a second sheet of plastic for the bottom of the cavity. But ordinarily the single sheet is all you will need.

Another tip: The best container for the still is made of plastic since it transmits heat. Metal cups and plates tend to collect heat themselves and so create their own evaporation process.

Some outfitters, particularly near the Southwest desert, sell solar stills, but you can easily make your own for only a modest cost.

The system for desert backpacking is to hike early in the morning, stay in the shade at midday, then hike again in the evening.

especially long hikes, caching more water at another location farther along. But this quickly becomes an expedition, not a form of recreation. However, it is a solution for a backpacking trip in an extremely hostile environment.

Each person's water requirements vary according to both his physiological and psychological makeup. Some people seem to travel like camels, needing very little water, while others seem to be sipping all the time. As a general rule—and a **very** general rule it is—a half-gallon per day will suffice for most people, providing none is wasted. If you must brush your teeth, for example, waste not a drop in rinsing the toothbrush. Use every bit of water for your body. Consume all, waste none.

In addition to guarding the water supply, you must also guard the supply already in your body so you won't waste it through perspiration. Desert backpacking is the place you must learn to amble or stroll rather than turn the trek into an endurance race and waste your body's supply of water through sweating.

A valuable lesson can be learned from the people who know more about the desert than anyone else—those who live in the deserts of Africa and Asia Minor. They wear clothing that completely covers their bodies, from head to ankle. The clothing is loose-fitting and usually of light color. It is lightweight and while it reflects much

of the sun's heat, it also helps conserve moisture by keeping the sun and wind away from the body so that the sun won't cause perspiration and the wind won't evaporate it so rapidly.

Thus it is important for us to wear loose-fitting clothing that covers most of the body. Some desert backpackers wear as little clothing as possible— shorts and a tee-shirt are almost a uniform for many backpackers. This is fine for early morning and late afternoon hiking when the heat is not so severe, but it is always better to wear clothing that covers.

Cotton is the best choice for desert clothing, just as it is one of the worst for cold-weather backpacking. It gives protection from the sun and wind, but does not trap air against the skin to increase and trap perspiration and heat. It is the poorest of the natural insulations and is thus best suited for desert clothing. The unbleached and simply-made baggy trousers and shirts worn by many Mexican peasants of years past were developed by the people who lived in the deserts of Northern Mexico because this was the best type of clothing for the climate, not because it was the only material and color available.

A carefully selected hat or cap is essential in the desert, with an emphasis on the hats with a reasonably broad brim. Hats offer protection for the whole head and neck, while caps do not. If a cap is worn, it must be supplemented with a light-colored bandana or other cloth for a neck covering.

Hats can be made of wool or any other material except straw, which does not give proper insulation from the sun and will not keep you warm at night or cool during the day. The hat you choose must have proper ventilation around the crown, either with holes that are in the hat when bought new, or those added by you with a punch, a grommet set, or simply a sharp knife or pair of scissors.

The best desert hats do not have an indention in the top to look rather stylish. This indention is a natural heat collector, and rainwater as well. Keep the crown pointed like that worn by World War I soldiers, or Smokey the Bear, to form a larger insulation barrier between the top of your head and the hat, and to give the sun and rain less surface on which to work.

A large bandana is always good for the neck. Old-time cowboys didn't wear them for decoration. They wore them for protection from the sun, to pull up over their faces to keep out sand and dust, and to dampen whenever possible to cool their necks. Remember that the blood vessels are close to the surface in the neck and scalp, and if the skin can be cooled there, it will help cool the rest of the body as well.

It is best to travel in the desert the first few hours of the morning and the last few hours of daylight, and then hole up under shelter during the heat of midday. If nothing else works, carry a small alarm clock to awake you at least an hour before daybreak so you can have your gear all assembled, a cup of hot chocolate, tea or coffee, and all your equipment on your back as soon as it is light enough to travel.

Most desert travelers, as noted earlier, walk at a leisurely gait to conserve energy and body liquids. It is best to stop frequently, at least every hour, to rest, cool off a bit and to take care of your feet since they are separated from the hot sand and rocks only by a very thin piece of leather and rubber. It is a good idea to take off your boots and socks at every stop to air them out and shake out any minute grains of sand that may have crept in. Perhaps you can change socks two or three times a day and let the others hang from the back of your pack to air out. Some desert travelers, such as Colin Fletcher, always give their feet a light bath in alcohol to both cool them and soothe them. Foot powder should also be used frequently to prevent rashes and keep the socks from clinging.

An experienced desert traveler will have a potential shelter spotted several minutes' hiking ahead to hole up during the heat of the day. This can be a pile of boulders that will soon be shaded by the afternoon sun, or beneath an overhang or simply a place to pitch the tent where the wind won't blow so strongly. Sometimes the midday shelter will be nothing more than a tarp, depending on the weather and location. But remember: If you pitch your tent, you must also pitch the rainfly, not only because the tent's fabric can be damaged by the sun's ultraviolet rays, but also because it helps create a heat barrier between the fly and tent walls.

When the heat lessens toward late afternoon, it is time to be off again, still at the slow and measured pace, and with the night's camp set up before darkness falls.

The desert has an undeserved

Unwelcome guests in campgrounds. From top, clockwise: rattlesnake, black widow spider, scorpion, and tarantula.

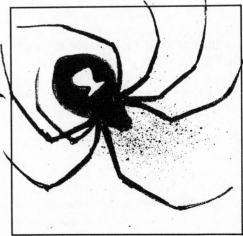

reputation for being a terrible place to visit and live. Part of that is due to the difficulty of living there, just as the Arctic is rugged for those who do not understand it or have no experience with it. And the desert is unduly feared because it has a few longtime residents with poisonuous stings or bites.

The most feared, and rightfully so, is the rattlesnake. Yet bites by them are extremely rare. They seldom if ever go out of their way to bite any mammal too large for them to eat. They bite people, burros, and mules, only when they are cornered, threatened or startled. They bite small animals and birds for food; they don't consider the rest of the animal kingdom as part of their food supply.

Thus, the way to avoid rattlesnake problems is to avoid places where rattlesnakes frequent. If you are walking through low brush, for example, give the brush a wide berth in case a snake is lying in the shade. Watch for sunlit places that are sheltered from the wind, such as behind rocks or along ledges. When you camp for the night, zip up the fly of your tent so the heat-seeking snakes can't come in to join you.

The one totally safe place from them is in the open sand where there is no protection from the sun. They function only at reasonable temperatures, and when the ground's surface reaches the upper 90°s F., they are in immediate danger of death. They function best between 80° and 90° F. Below that they become sluggish, and above it they will die if they don't find shade.

Scorpions are another problem, but not a serious one if you don't turn over stones, and if you do, look before reaching. They are more of a problem around populated areas than in the

---

BACKPACKER'S TIP

Light-colored desert sand reflects back up to 80% of the light that falls on it—that's almost as much reflection as snow. Desert and seashore trips demand that sun-glasses be worn, even on cloudy days. Unprotected eyes soon become inflamed; they burn, water, and make the head ache. Treatment is aspirin for pain and a cold compress on the eyes. Patient should wear a light-proof bandage or stay in a dark shelter. Eye drops or ointments are not recommended.

---

desert, and almost never in the open desert because they, too, need shade from the sun.

If you camp near a rockfall or boulders, you may have scorpions for company during the cooler hours. But if you don't make a habit of picking up things from the ground without first kicking them with your booted foot, or using a stick to first turn them over, your chances of meeting a scorpion on his terms are slight. Their sting is invariably painful, and in the case of two small species in Arizona, can be fatal.

Again, keep your tent flap zipped at all times, and look inside your boots before putting them on if they've been outside the tent long. Better yet, keep them in the tent at all times when not in use.

The other major villain of the desert is the spider, such as the black widow and tarantula. See Chapter 16 for information on them.

To repeat, most desert backpackers never see any of these fearful creatures, and experienced desert travelers take their presence for granted to the extent that their method of traveling and living in the desert leaves little or no opportunity for being surprised by—or surprising—these creatures.

Down and other cold-weather insulators will also work to a limited degree against heat. So when you are carrying an extra canteen in your pack, wrap it in your down or synthetic insulated parka, or inside your sleeping bag, and it will remain cool longer.

CHAPTER 13

ROUTE FINDING

Nearly every backpacker who has gone off the beaten track a few times will eventually admit to having been confused at one time or another—even more than confused but struck by that momentary panic that accompanies the fact that you don't know where you are. This can happen anywhere—in the middle of a dense forest, on an open plain or desert, or even in a large urban park. Virtually everyone who wanders from their home base becomes disoriented at some time. Remember the time you flew into a strange city at night, woke up the next morning, and looked out the hotel window and saw the sun coming up in the **west?** You weren't lost—you knew where you were—but you were certainly disoriented.

This happens frequently on backpacking trips, especially when the trail winds up and down and around peaks, boulders, or low ridges. Suddenly you stop, look around more carefully, and realize you don't have the vaguest idea of where you are or if you are even walking in the right direction. This also happens easily on cloudy days or just at evening when the sun has disappeared behind the peaks and you have no light-and-shadow effect for orientation.

In nearly every such case, the hiker will stop, take inventory, mentally go back over the route, and—unless panic has set in—reestablish one's general whereabouts, and continue on. Strangely, this frequently happens only a few yards short of the goal or the campsite. The hour is late, the campsite farther away than anticipated, and fatigue is now a factor.

There are ways to avoid letting this happen to you. One is always—**always**—to be sure you know where you are and to know which direction you're supposed to be walking. The best way to prevent getting confused is to have a map along, preferably a topographical map that you have studied well in advance of the trip and to which you refer frequently while you hike along.

As an example, you are hiking several miles across rolling terrain that is interspersed with open country and wooded bottoms. Your topographical map shows the dominant features along the way—peaks, manmade structures, such as buildings and roads, gullies and ravines, and so forth. As you studied the map before the trip, you noted the dominant features you would find all along the route, such as hills you will have to climb, junctions of streams or stream beds, and elevation gains or losses. And as you hike along the route, refer constantly to the map to identify these checkpoints. Stop frequently, turn around, and check the points behind you with those on the map. Always know to within a few hundred feet exactly where you are.

Although you will do most of your backpacking along well-established and maintained trails, you should still know exactly where you are so you can have some basis for estimating your time of arrival. The eight miles you hiked yesterday in only four hours may be a breeze compared with the five miles you have to hike today through windfallen timber, up and down ravines, and around gullies that are too deep for scrambling. Today's five miles may actually be more like yesterday's eight or nine because of all the detours and the up-and-down nature of the route.

By knowing how to read a topographical map properly, you can avoid such unpleasant surprises. When you see a series of contour lines crowded together so tightly that they almost touch, you know you are looking at a cliff or some reasonable facsimile of one, and you will want to choose another route.

Sometimes the features shown on topographical maps aren't dominant enough to be easily recognized when you see them in reality, such as when you're hiking across broken ground with no taller mountains or manmade features around. Everything tends to look alike, both on the map and in reality. This is one of those times you definitely need a compass and to know how to read it as well as your wrist watch.

COMPASS

Reduced to its simplest definition, a compass is a needle balanced on a pin, with one end of the needle magnetized so that it always points toward magnetic north. Not the North Pole, but the **Magnetic** North Pole. This is an important distinction because the Magnetic North Pole is actually in northeastern Canada, roughly 1,000 miles south of the North Pole.

The magnetized compass needle is mounted on the free-wheeling pin above a dial that shows all the major directions—and often is marked with the 360° of a circle as well. Nearly all compasses are covered with a plastic dial for protection. On some models this cover can be turned and has an arrow printed on it to represent true north (toward the North Pole).

All maps are based on the North and South Poles, since the poles are the only geographic constants in direction-finding. Other constants for direction-finding, unrelated to topographical maps and compasses, are found in the stars, the sun, and the moon—elements of celestial navigation.

If a direct line is drawn from the true North Pole down through the Magnetic North Pole and then extended south, a magnetic compass needle held somewhere on that extended line will point true north. For any other location, the compass needle will point to some lesser or greater degree away from true north. Therefore, compasses and maps must have adjustments to allow for the differences in the locations of these two poles. This angle of difference between the two poles is called "declination." It varies in different parts of North America, and all United States and Canadian top-

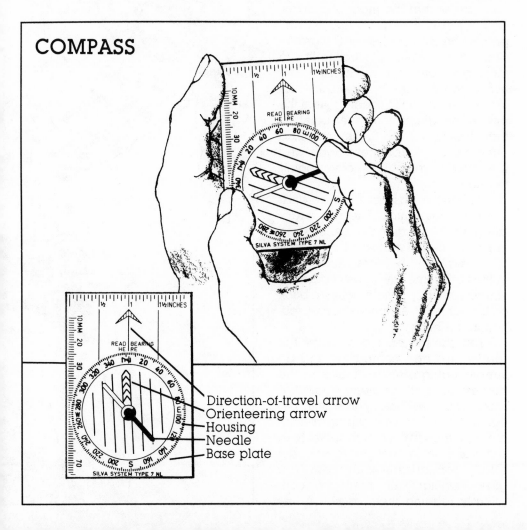

COMPASS

Direction-of-travel arrow
Orienteering arrow
Housing
Needle
Base plate

ographical maps have the angle of declination printed on them. Be aware, also, that the magnetic pole wanders a bit, perhaps a degree a year. So be certain your maps are up to date, showing the declination recently.

This is where the clear plastic covers on the better compasses are a necessity. To use your compass properly, you first consult the map you're using and find the angle of declination printed on it close to where the arrow pointing north is seen. This angle is stated in degrees. Then you hold the compass so that the magnetic arrow points north directly over "North" printed on the dial below the arrow. Count the degrees of declination in the proper direction away from true north, and turn the clear plastic dial above the magnetic needle so that the printed needle on the cover points in that direction. Now the magnetized needle points to magnetic north, and the printed arrow on the cover points to true north.

This is the basis of all map-and-compass navigation. The rest is applied simple mathematics, easy to learn. It is best to start with basics after reading a few instructions. Usually such instructions come with the compass, but you can also buy a more-detailed book on the subject (see the Resources section in this book).

You can largely teach yourself to read maps and compasses and do simple navigation exercises in the nearest city park or along a familiar route. This is especially true with becoming familiar with topographical maps. Both maps and compasses take some familiarization before you feel totally comfortable with them. You grow familiar with maps by consciously reading them as you travel

along highways, backroads, and well-established trail systems. Watch for landmarks and compare them with the map.

Most backpackers seldom have a use for a compass, since they usually hike on established trails, occasionally checking their maps, and so have a general idea of the distance they have traveled and the distance yet to

compass. And you will need to refer to them frequently. This is also true if you walk in a heavy fog, a cloudburst, or at night. Under the best of circumstances, you're already in trouble if you are hiking at night, and you will need the compass to confirm that you are headed in the right direction.

One of the primary rules of brush-beating or cross-country travel is "never

go before reaching their goal. A compass is a necessity when traveling over land without roads or trails. An occasional check with the compass tells you if you've wandered off the direction you're headed, and, if so, how far or how many degrees.

However, if you are traveling in a vast wilderness system, such as in Canada or Alaska, where no trails exist and where few streams flow, such as in the lake country of the vast interior of Canada; you need both maps and

lose elevation unnecessarily," meaning that when you can stay on ridges or otherwise higher ground, do so. You can spot landmarks easier, and your labors will be lessened by avoiding scrambling in and out of canyons.

Another equally obvious rule is to find game trails heading in your direction and to stay with them, if possible. Animals are no more energetic than mankind; when an animal can find a path of least resistance, it will do so.

WAYS TO FIND NORTH

If you're not carrying a compass (and you should always carry one) and you need to find north, there are a variety of ways to do so. You might not find true north precisely, but these methods will at least give you a very close direction so that you're not heading west or east, or even south, when you want true north.

One way is to use a pole and length of string—a boot lace will suffice.

Push a pole or straight stick into the ground and be sure it is vertical. Make a plumb bob of a string and stone or your pocketknife, if necessary. Then make a loose loop in the string so it will slide evenly around the stick, slip it over, and let it drop to the base of the stick. Draw a half circle with a second stick at the other end of the string starting at the tip of the present shadow the center stick throws. Drive a stick into the ground at this point.

Watch the shadow. It will shorten until it is noon by local standard—not daylight savings—time. Watch for the

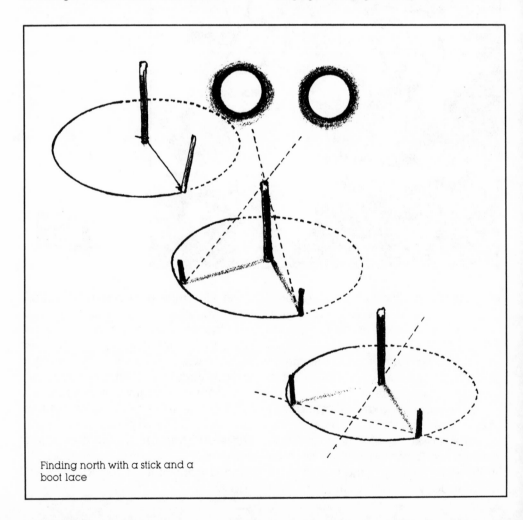

Finding north with a stick and a boot lace

moment the shadow again reaches the half-circle line you have drawn. Mark this point with another stick.

Draw a line connecting the pole with the point halfway between the first and second shadow marks. This halfway point and the pole will be in direct line with true north.

Another method using shadows is equally effective and faster and works with either the sun or moon.

Drive a stick perfectly vertical as before. Mark the top of the shadow with a pebble or twig. Wait a few minutes, five or ten is best, and mark the tip of the new shadow. A line joining the first with the second mark will point west. You can then take it from there. Remember, though, that in most of North America the line will run a bit to the south of west in the morning, and in the afternoon it will run somewhat north of west.

You can also use your watch as a compass. First, if you are on daylight saving time, move the watch back an hour to sun time. Then take a wooden matchstick or something similar and place the watch on a level surface with the sun hitting it. Hold the match so

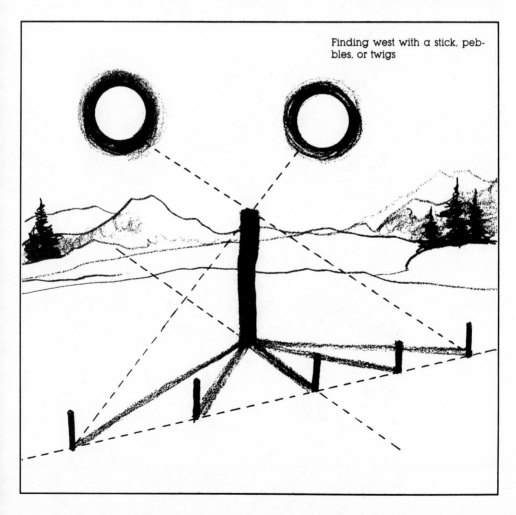

Finding west with a stick, pebbles, or twigs

that it is exactly in the center of the watch and is vertical. Turn the watch until the stick's shadow is along the hour hand.

If you do this between 6:00 A.M. and 6:00 P.M., south will be directly between the hour hand and 12:00 on the watch in the angle formed by the two hands. If you're doing this between 6:00 P.M. and 6:00 A.M., north will be between the hour hand and 12:00.

The formula to remember is N for North and Night, S for South and Sun (daytime).

CHAPTER 14

COOKING

Barring disasters or meeting the girl or boy of your dreams in the wilderness, the quality of food is usually the most memorable part of a backpacking trip. This is especially true if the food is poor or if you didn't bring enough and had to spend the last day on a forced march without rations. On the other hand, if that beef stroganoff you prepared the second night out was spectacular, you will probably remember that as well as you do the waterfall where you took a delightful shower or the thunderstorm that missed your camp by three or four miles but gave you an exciting afternoon.

Thus, it is no surprise that the old chestnut about an army traveling on its stomach is so tried and true. No other animal comfort quite takes the place of a delicious meal, a cup of hot cocoa, or that first cup of steaming coffee in the morning.

Fortunately the days are long gone when you had to carry canned meats and vegetables, and you were constantly tempted to overeat the first day or two simply to lighten the load and be rid of those lumps in your pack.

Food manufacturers have not been remiss in seizing upon the backpacking fraternity as a prime market for its freeze-dried and dehydrated foods: everything from the fruit juice before breakfast to coffee and tea, and on through the meats, vegetables, and sauces. Modern backpacking foods weigh only a tenth as much as they used to, thanks to these two methods of preserving and reducing food weight. Instead of opening three cans and worrying about ptomaine, today you can buy prepackaged dinners for two to six that weigh no more than a paperback book and take up only a little more space in your pack.

The variety of food that lends itself to lightweight travel is almost endless. If you don't like the way food is offered in the popular prepackaged lunches and dinners, you can buy a deyhdrator and do it yourself. Grocery-store shelves are laden with lightweight and compact foods. Anything you find that has directions for reconstitution, from sauces to spaghetti, is a candidate for your backpacking trip. Individual tastes and your imagination are the only restrictions.

BACKPACKER'S TIP

One way to reduce the bulk of powdered substances, such as milk and pancake batter, is to run it through your blender. This will reduce the volume by as much as forty percent.

Some backpackers on short trips— no more than a weekend—do away with cooking entirely and take stoves along (if they take them at all) for hot drinks only. You can load up on nuts, sausages, cheese, jerky, seeds, bread, dried fruits, crackers, and freeze-dried vegetables and eat them just the way they are.

But if you plan a longer trip, you can't depend on uncooked foods alone because the troops will rebel if the gastronomic tract doesn't do so first. Uncooked, cold food quickly wears out its welcome. Before long you yearn for a hot meal, even mush, that you can smell bubbling away over a stove for several minutes before it is eaten. The sheer animal comfort of a hot meal does wonders for one's mental well being.

If you tend to treat food simply as fuel for the body—with no concern for those extra little touches that make beef stroganoff a culinary experience—then the prepackaged meals will greatly simplify your trip planning. These meals are composed of individual packages of freeze-dried or dehydrated components for two to six persons, and all are then enclosed in a sturdy plastic bag. This is the simple, no-nonsense approach to menu planning.

Most backpackers prefer to organize their own meals more completely. Outdoor stores usually stock a good supply of lighweight foods, ranging from hamburgers to eggs to cobbler. You can find all forms of meat, vegetables, drinks, and desserts, packaged in a variety of servings. Thus, you can make up your daily menus and go shopping in outdoor stores much as you would a supermarket, knowing that whatever is available will be small and light.

Obviously, supermarkets have other items that outdoor stores might not stock, such as the various soups, sauce mixes, spices, and other specialty items.

Since food processing has improved so much in the past decade in favor of lightweight and compact traveling, the question has changed from how to find the food to how to select it. With this in mind, here are a few suggestions for each meal.

BREAKFAST

Unless you are staying at one site for more than a night, you will want a simple, quick-cook breakfast that won't interfere with breaking camp and getting back on the trail. Nor will you want to spend much time cleaning up after the meal. Many backpackers simply heat one pot filled with water and use it for hot drinks, followed with oatmeal that is eaten in the same cup (usually a Sierra cup), which is then rinsed out and reused for the second cup of coffee or tea while getting the pack ready.

Or you can have a cup of orange or grapefruit juice made from powdered mixes, a cup of cereal made with powdered milk, then the hot drinks such as coffee, hot chocolate, or tea. Again, only one stove and one pot is required. Save a bit of hot water to rinse out the cup and clean the spoon.

Then pack away the stove and you are ready to go.

Eggs mixed with bacon bars, melba toast, and the drinks are also possible by using a few more minutes for preparation and cleanup.

Some of the more hard-nosed backpackers bound out of the sleeping bag, stow everything into the pack, head out on the trail with a plastic bag of granola or granola bars, and hike an hour or two before stopping for hot drinks. But most people prefer to face the day with the memory of hot drinks and a more familiar breakfast behind them.

As the sample menu in this chapter shows, you can have a different breakfast each day without wasting a lot of time around the cooking area. Unless you have a blister, you will be anxious to head out each morning without a lot of time spent scrubbing pots and utensils.

LUNCH

Usually this is the only cold meal of the day, although it certainly isn't mandatory that it be cold. It is just simpler. If you are addicted to hot drinks, one of the group's stoves can be pulled from a pack and water heated while the lunch items—cheese, fruit, peanut butter, pemmican bars, or whatever—are distributed. If the weather is warm, you will probably make cold drinks from packaged mixes. If you are hiking in cool weather, soups and hot drinks will be appreciated.

Often you will not be very hungry for lunch, especially if you have been nibbling throughout the morning on your gorp, beef jerky, or other snack items. Lunch provides a good excuse to get the pack off your back for half an hour while you stretch out beside the trail and watch the clouds and listen to the wind or the silence.

Whatever the case, it is best to keep lunch as simple as breakfast, if not more so. There will always be one or more members of your group who rank hiking over eating, so keep them happy by spending as little time as possible preparing the first two meals of the day.

DINNER

Unless you have misjudged the distance you will hike each day, or someone has appropriated your planned campsite, you should stop for the night while you still have lots of daylight left. This gives you time to prepare the meal at a leisurely pace, clean up afterwards, and still have daylight for strolling around the area or simply for reading the paperback you brought along.

Dinner can be rather elaborate. Careful planning permits you to cook it on one stove and with one pot. Drinks, perhaps an appetizer first, a hot soup,

---

BACKPACKER'S TIP

Sometimes your backpacking stove becomes overheated when a large pot has been on it for a while as it reflects the heat downward onto the fuel tank. A good way to avoid this is to wrap the stove in aluminum foil to reflect the heat upward off the stove and back onto the pot.

vegetables, meat, and an easily prepared dessert will make the evening
a success. Hot chocolate toward bedtime is still another bonus.

Or you can splurge and use two
stoves and several pots for this meal.
By using more pots, you can also afford to give the troops a choice of main
courses. Some may not be enthralled
with spaghetti and meatballs, in which
case you can let them have beef stroganoff or a hearty stew.

By making dinner more of an
event, you give everyone something
to look forward to each day. And this
is especially true when backpacking
with young children who lose interest
in scenery rather quickly when they
are hungry. Even dedicated backpackers tend to experience a dropoff
in interest in the wilderness after a few
days; the prospect of excellent food
helps them get through each day. It is
something on the order of a carrot on
the proverbial stick.

ONE-BURNER
COOKING

With only a little planning, you can
readily cook all meals on a single-
burner stove, using two pots that pack
nested into each other. Under this ar-
rangement you use one pot to heat
water while using the other for cooking. Here are some suggestions on how
to do this:

- In one pot get the water heating for
  the first beverage.
- When the water is warm, pour some
  into the second pot to rehydrate
  soup.
- As soon as you've used the rest of

the water for the first beverage, start
another course, such as a casserole,
in the first pot.
- Switch pots on the burner, boil the
  soup, and eat it.
- Then switch pots and bring the casserole or stew to boil and eat.

Rinse the soup pot and start with fresh
water for second beverage or
dessert.

In this manner, not only does the
cook have a chance to eat with the
rest of the group, but the stove is being
used at all times and no time or effort
or fuel is wasted.

Most packstoves have a burning
capacity limited to little more than an
hour. By keeping the stove in use constantly, most meals can be prepared
during the burning time of one tank.
It is a nuisance to have to stop cooking
and refill the tank because the stove
must be cooled first. Then, there is always the possibility of spilling fuel on
your hands or food.

WHAT SIZE POT?

Although backpacking cooksets
come in reasonably standard sizes,
many are determined by the kind of
stove that will nest inside them for carrying. Here are a few suggestions on
how to determine the size(s) you need
for your group:

Add up the number of cups of
water needed to serve the meal and
beverages. For four persons—4 cups
for soup, 4 for coffee or tea, 4 for casserole, 4 for second cup of hot drink.
This equals 16 cups, or eight pints, or
4 quarts. This can be done with two 2-
quart pots, but it's easier with one 2-
quart pot and one 3- or 4-quart pot.

MINIMUM-IMPACT OUTDOOR COOKING

The more efficient you become in cooking, the less impact you have on the environment, and the easier it will be for everyone in your group. This means that you will avoid heat damage to living things, that you won't create garbage problems, that you won't turn the campsite into a quagmire or create new trails to the water source, and also that nobody will have to spend an inordinate amount of time around the campstove.

Other than the environmental-protection arguments against roaring campfires, the best argument for cooking over a packstove is that it is more efficient. You have more control over the heat and a packstove is faster to operate.

Here are some arguments in favor of packstove cookery:

■ Open fires are at the mercy of the

BACKPACKER'S TIP

Dark-colored pots bring water to boil faster than bright, shiny ones, because they absorb rather than reflect heat from the stove. More and more pots are being sold in dark colors for this reason—or at least blackened on the bottom.

weather. Fried food is often burnt or soggy. Rehydration of freeze-dried foods is often cut short, causing a chain reaction of indigestion and undeveloped flavors.

- Packstoves do not cause smoke in your face and on your clothing and do not result in ember holes burned in nylon clothing, tents, and packs.
- You avoid devoting too much time to gathering wood, nursing the fire along, chopping wood, and trying to start a fire with wet or green wood. A packstove gives you all of this time to do other, more enjoyable things in camp.
- Wood fires scatter ashes in all of your camping gear, as well as create blackened pots and pans.

STOVES

Compact and lightweight stoves have come as close as any outdoor equipment to reaching a state of the art; it is difficult to imagine their becoming smaller and lighter than they already are, or more dependable. Some of the old-faithful models that are still with us are a bit complicated to operate, and some backpackers are comforted by their old ones because they feel a certain loyalty to them, actually enjoying the ritual of coaxing them to life under severe and pleasant weather conditions. This is especially true of certain European manufactured stoves that have earned their place in the annals of mountaineering and polar exploration.

The basic design of stoves has changed little over the years. And you won't go wrong by buying any of the models you've read about in accounts of men and women who have lived under extreme weather conditions, depending on their stoves for food and drink to warm and nourish the body.

Stoves use three basic fuels: white gas (or naphtha), propane and butane, and kerosene. Very few campers use kerosene stoves in North

---

BACKPACKER'S TIP

Although pancakes (or flapjacks or hot cakes or whatever you care to call them) are a popular item in camps, they are not the simplest item for backpacking. The batter takes up both space and weight; you need a sturdy (meaning heavy) skillet or pan for them; and they take more time to prepare than the add-boiling-water breakfast foods.

America; it is the least popular fuel due to its unpleasant odor, its susceptibility to smoking and to staining pots and pans, and the difficulty in coaxing it into flame because of its low octane rating. It is, however, perhaps the only truly international fuel—kerosene is available in remote villages where butane or propane have never been heard of. For all practical purposes, though, it is not a high-priority fuel in North America.

This leaves white gas (we'll use it as an umbrella word to cover naphtha, Blazo, and Coleman fuels) and butane and propane, both of which are stored in pressurized containers.

Of these two varieties, the white gas stoves are probably the most common among backpackers because of the two factors all back-

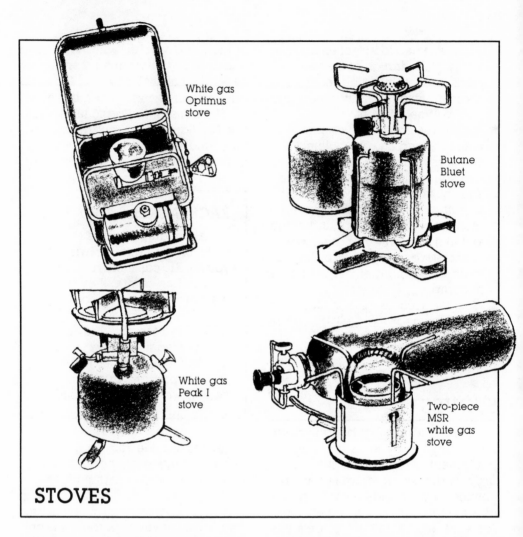

White gas
Optimus
stove

Butane
Bluet
stove

White gas
Peak I
stove

Two-piece
MSR
white gas
stove

STOVES

packers must worry about—space and weight. A pint of white gas, plus a stove tank full, will last through several meals. The same amount of cooking time with butane and propane cartridges will occupy much more space in your pack and much more weight. Also, the cartridges must be carried with you whether empty or full, while white gas stoves will lighten your load as the fuel is consumed.

White gas stoves are manufactured in two categories: those that must be preheated before they will produce a flame, and those that are

equipped with pressure pumps that force the fuel to vaporize and so produce instant flame.

Those that must be preheated call for a bit of dexterity by the camp cook. The usual method of starting them is to clean the burner first—many models require a portable cleaner that you carry with the stove, or new models have the burner cleaner built into the control valve. After the tiny nozzle of the burner is cleaned, a small amount of white gas or alcohol is poured into the burner area and then ignited. While this fuel burns, the burner is getting hot

One of the newer lightweight stoves attaches to a butane or propane tank, and weighs only ounces.

EDDIE BAUER ON DRINKING WATER

"I've had unpleasant experiences from drinking 'back country' well water. Often it is contaminated. The well owner and his family have built up immunity? Visitors?...perhaps yes...perhaps no. Why take a chance on spoiling your trip? Carry your water with you from a reliable source—like your home tap."

enough to vaporize the fuel as it comes up from the tank. The flame is blue and white—and cooking hot.

These preheating stoves can become somewhat cranky, and their owners soon develop highly personal rituals for coaxing them into life. Some disdain the use of a medicine dropper to place the fuel in the burner bowl for preheating. Instead, they open the valve, then cradle the stove in their hands until their body heat seeps through the fuel tank and causes the fuel to expand and overflow into the burner bowl. Then they turn off the valve and light the fuel.

The mainstay of family campers

who operate from their cars or pack animals has always been the Coleman stove, one so popular and familiar that there seems to be no other way to describe it except as a Coleman. These stoves have a pump built onto the fuel tank; and after a specified number of strokes of the pump, the stove is almost invariably ready to be lit.

SOME KITCHEN SUGGESTIONS

- **Stove kit**: It should be the right size for the number in the party. Check the kind of stove you buy for the number of servings easily prepared on it. Some are suitable for two or three, others for four or six at one serving.
- **A good work base**: This is essential for safety, for avoiding spillage, and for the cook's good spirits. Some backpackers carry a piece of plywood about the size of a sheet of typing paper as a base. One-fourth inch plywood this size weighs little and takes very little space in your pack. A cookie tin or piece of aluminum will serve the same function.
- **A light tarp**: The cooking area should have shade from the sun and a roof during rain. A lightweight piece of waterproof nylon with grommets can be fashioned into a sunshade or rain fly very easily.

Backpacking pump stoves operate on the same theory, except in much smaller proportions. These stoves are folded into their own case—and are not much larger or heavier than the plastic sandwich boxes so popular at fast-food establishments. Open the lid, stroke the pump, apply a match, and you have a stove capable of feeding multitudes. None of the Aladdin-style rubbing is required to bring it to life.

Relatively new stoves come in components, so that the fuel tank of the stove itself is no longer necessary. These stoves are simply a burner attached to the fuel bottle via a hose and valve, cutting down on weight even further, although the savings is in ounces rather than pounds.

Each design has its own advantages and disadvantages, and much depends on each individual's preferences. But the matter of fuel selection is a bit more clear cut because the kind of backpacking you do, and the weather conditions, largely determine the type of fuel you will use.

White gas burns anywhere, in any weather condition and any altitude. Butane- and propane-powered stoves are not so basic. Butane will not vaporize at freezing level, whereas propane isn't so severely affected by cold. A disposable butane cartridge provides up to three hours of burning. Propane must be stored at a higher pressure than butane, and the cartridge is heavier as a result. Both must be stored in the shade to avoid overpressurization, which can cause the safety valve to release. There are good alcohol stoves available, but alcohol doesn't provide as much heat as other fuels.

Several other camp tools have been adapted to propane and butane. Small lanterns can be attached to the tops of the cartridges to give out a bright light. Compact and lightweight griddles, two-burner stoves, and a wide variety of other cooking, heating, and lighting products are available that are powered by the cartridges.

Conversely, most white-gas lanterns and implements are still on the bulky side.

For many backpackers, the weight and bulk of the cartridges are more than offset by the ease of operation with butane and propane. No priming, no preheating. Simply turn on the valve, light and adjust, and you have instant heat. And usually much quieter heat. Some white-gas stoves are quiet, but most emit a hiss—or a roar.

Since weight and space are the two major concerns for backpacking, it is best to buy nesting cooksets so that your stove, pots, implements (cleaning tools, spare parts, and lifting handles) all fit inside each other with no space wasted. Some of these cooksets have three or more pots (you can get by with a maximum of two pots), a base for the stove, and a place for the stove itself so it won't rattle around inside the pots.

As stoves range from old-fashioned to the-state-of-the-art, the final decision on which kind you buy becomes one of personal preference, and even emotion. Some people simply like white-gas stoves because they have such a long tradition in extreme conditions, even though they may not be as easy to operate or as quiet as the compressed-gas stoves. Other backpackers who don't enjoy fiddling with equipment—who want to set up the stove, light it, and forget it—will in turn be attracted to the butane and pro-

pane types. Each has its own limitations and each has its own advantages. The choice is yours.

STOVE SAFETY

To avoid being burned, it is a good idea to wear a pair of inexpensive gloves while cooking. Many backpackers carry a pair of pliers to use as potholders, to adjust stoves with hot

ELEVATED COOKING

A good rule of thumb on estimating cooking time at various elevations is to assume that cooking time will double at each additional 5,000 feet above sea level. You should remember this when planning meals, because all recipes are written for sea-level cooking.

This chart shows the temperature at which water boils at different elevations, topping off at 10,000 feet under the assumption that few backpackers will be much higher. Above 10,000 feet, you're usually climbing, not backpacking, unless you're tramping down the Rocky Mountain crest in Wyoming or Colorado.

Altitude	°F	°C
Sea Level	212	100
2,000 feet	208	98
5,000 feet	203	95
10,000 feet	194	90

COOKING WITH HERBS AND SPICES

Since nearly all freeze-dried and dehydrated foods are prepared institutionally bland to avoid offending various tastes, you have to add your own seasonings and other additives to suit your own taste. Although few of these additives have any nutritional value, their aesthetic value to an otherwise bland meal cannot be overemphasized.

Most cooks agree that no dish should taste so strongly that the original flavor is lost. Thus, when using sage and garlic, remember that they tend to dominate after cooking. But milder seasonings such as thyme, marjoram, and other aromatics will tend to "cook out" and be lost. Thus, you will have to add a pinch (for four persons) shortly before the end of the cooking period in order to enjoy the flavor.

Spices have other uses in trail cooking as well. They have a tendency to help preserve food by slowing the oxidation of edible fats that turn them rancid. And some do assist in digestion, while at the same time correct the tendency of certain foods to produce flatulence.

Spices commonly used in tropical countries to slow oxidation include the chilies, cumin, caraway, fennel, cinnamon, nutmeg, cloves, pepper, turmeric, and others.

Following is a list of spices and their suggested uses:

Allspice: Baked fruit desserts, sweet potatoes, spaghetti sauce, and corned beef.

Basil: All soups and sauces, all tomato dishes, stews, and in mixtures with parsley and the aromatic seasonings.

Bay Leaf: All beef dishes, stews, stuffings, and pickles.

Borage: This is a common wild plant good with salads.

Caraway seeds: Goulash, chicken stew, fish chowder, and sour cream sauce.

Chilies (red peppers): All tropical foods (and a good source of vitamins A and C).

Cinnamon: Baked fruit desserts, Hungarian chicken, and sweet vegetables.

Cloves: Same and also in various teas.

Cumin: With chilies, in eggs, curries, and cheeses.

Curry: A mixture of various spices that may be used in many ways, such as with meats.

File (Sassafras): Creole gumbo with aromatics and vegetables.

Ginger: (Keep fresh) Has many uses in meats, vegetables, and pastries.

Horseradish: Roast beef and oily fish, shrimp sauce, and salad dressings.

Marjoram: "When in doubt, try marjoram." One of the aromatics.

Nutmeg: Pastries, vegetables, and meats. A "sweet" spice.

Oregano: Many Italian dishes. A "warm" aromatic.

Paprika: A sweet taste that is high in vitamin C.

Parsley: Can be used in anything.

Rosemary: Another aromatic. Steep leaves before using and put in dish late in cooking period.

Saffron: High in vitamin B-2 and aids in digestion of fatty foods; also very expensive.

Tarragon: A "must" in French cookery.

Thyme: Another "must" for French dishes, poultry, and fish.

Vanilla: The most popular flavor in the world and is emphasized in desserts.

How do you carry and use spices in lightweight cooking for backpacking trips?

The best thing is to make up a gourmet kit. This will be a very small kit containing vials and plastic containers of your favorite spices and seasonings. The kit, which will be no larger than a paperback book when folded into a convenient package, can contain several spices, sauce mixes, broth for stock, dry soups and gravies, and small amounts of oil, vinegar, and cooking wine.

Basic menus for backpackers are usually based on freeze-dried meats sold in two-ounce packages—beef, ham, chicken, sausage, and so forth. The nutrition unit is usually one ounce per person per day, which means that one package of meat can go into a meal for three or four persons, with other foods throughout the day making up the difference. Fat has been removed from freeze-dried meats, so about one teaspoon of margarine or butter should be added to give the fat the body requires.

If you are backpacking in an area that has good fishing, you can supplement part of your diet by catching fish and preparing them in a gourmet manner, such as Trout Almondine. But you shouldn't assume you're going to catch fish and plan your menu around your fishing abilities. Too many anglers come home empty-handed to make this a dependable source of food.

EDDIE BAUER ON FOOD/STOVES/FIRES

"Because they are light in weight, give an instantaneous cooking flame, and produce controllable heat, most backpackers today carry packstoves that burn white gas, butane, propane, or alcohol. Wood fires are forbidden in an increasing number of campgrounds. Where you see fire pits, you will probably find that firewood is available through the ranger's office. You can leave your saw and axe at home because cutting firewood is forbidden. It's not far away when open fires will be in the 'emergency only' category."

HEAT INTENSIFIERS

Some packstoves come with wind screens, which also serve as heat intensifiers or are built into the cookset designed to fit particular stoves. Others are not, and you waste a lot of heat without them. You can build a simple one out of lightweight aluminum sheeting that can be formed into a box that folds flat in your pack, or aluminum cylinders that fit inside a pot for packing. Whichever you choose, they are worth it in time and fuel saved.

valves, and for a variety of other uses. Pliers are one of the most versatile tools you can find for camping.

Never overfill fuel tanks in pack stoves. The intake of the safety valve will then be below the surface of the fuel, which could overheat and squirt out during preheating to turn your stove into a wild blow torch. Also, stoves need air space for pressurization.

Denatured alcohol is safer for preheating stoves than stove fuel. A small vial will usually last through most backpacking trips.

If your stove starts acting strangely, either torching or sputtering, throw cold water on it to reduce the internal pressure and to cool the valve so you can shut it off safely.

SOME FAVORITE BACKPACKING RECIPES

HOT COCOA MIX

Combine:

2 cups powdered milk
¼ cup cocoa
1 cup powdered sugar with dash of salt
⅓ cup powdered non-dairy creamer
1 or 2 tablespoons malted milk powder (only if you like malt flavor)

To mix: Put 4 tablespoons of mix into a cup of boiling water. Add a miniature marshmallow, if desired.

FRUIT-NUT ENERGY BAR

3-¾ cups whole wheat flour
1 cup sugar
1 cup instant nonfat dry milk
½ cup wheat germ
2 teaspoons baking powder
4 eggs
2 cups water
¾ cup vegetable oil
½ cup honey
½ cup molasses
2 cups seedless raisins
1½ cups (8 ounces) snipped dried apricots (or mixed fruit)
1 cup sunflower seeds

Preheat oven to 350°. Combine all ingredients in a large bowl; mix well.

Pour into a greased large (jelly-roll size) pan. Bake in a 350° oven for 45–55 minutes. Cool and cut into bars. Bars will keep 3–4 days on the trail, indefinitely in a freezer.

FRUITED SEED BARS

Combine:

1 cup sesame seeds
½ cup chopped nuts
½ cup sunflower or pumpkin seeds
 —toast as directed on package (usually 10-15 minutes at 350°)

In a 10″–12″ fry pan, combine:

½ cup honey
½ cup firmly packed brown sugar
¼ teaspoon salt
½ cup chopped dried fruit

Bring mixture to a boil over medium heat, stirring constantly; cook 2 minutes. Remove pan from heat and immediately stir in seeds and nuts and ½ cup unsweetened shredded coconut; mix thoroughly. Follow directions above. Let cool 30 minutes before removing from pan.

BACKPACKER'S TIP

The shelf life of most freeze-dried and dehydrated foods is 18 to 24 months, if they are properly packaged so that air and moisture cannot enter the package. Two or three days is the maximum time you should allow food to be consumed after opening. Thus, if you have leftover and opened food after a backpacking trip, you should either eat it at home or put it in a freezer until the next trip—and then be certain it is the first food eaten on that trip.

GRANOLA

Although granola has been discovered by virtually every food manufacturer and grocery-store shelves are laden with granola bars containing chocolate, peanut butter, and virtually every fattening product known to mankind, still it is possible to find granola that is as nutritious as it is tasty. Or you can make your own:

4 cups quick-cooking oatmeal
2½ cups wheat germ
1 cup coconut
½ cup sunflower seeds
½ cup other nuts (almonds, walnuts, cashews, and so forth)
1 teaspoon cinnamon
2 tablespoons brown sugar

Heat the following—do not bring to boil—and stir into the above mixture:

½ cup honey
½ cup salad oil
1 teaspoon vanilla

Spread into big baking pan. Bake in slow oven 325° 20–30 minutes, stirring every ten minutes. Bake until golden brown. Remove and add raisins and mixed dried fruit, as desired. Cut into bars and wrap in plastic. Can be stored in the freezer almost indefinitely.

FIRES

Not too many years ago no one gave much thought to building campfires, and the idea that campfires would one day (today) be considered taboo in the wilderness was too strange to ponder. But when the camping and backpacking fever caught on in North America, it soon became an epidemic that shows no signs of lessening. One direct result is the almost total disappearance of abundant firewood in nearly every national forest and other public lands. Only in national parks, where restrictions were placed early, can you find the forests in their native state with fallen trees, branches, and bark decomposing to nurture the forests and provide both food and lodging for many of the insects and small animals that make up important links in the food chain.

Popular trails became pocked with unsightly fire rings and fire pits, most of which killed the vegetation several inches down in the soil. Clearly, man's instinctive need for a blazing fire at night—perhaps a need stored in our genes from times prehistoric—has had to take another step upward in the evolutionary sequence. Now we are told, and with very good reason, to avoid campfires while traveling in the wilderness.

This has been a bitter pill for many backpackers to swallow because more than tramping along the trail . . . more than sunrises in high places . . . more than sleeping beneath the stars . . . sitting around the campfire in

---

BACKPACKER'S TIP

Generally speaking, dehydrated foods do not prepare as successfully as freeze-dried. They are shrunken as well as dried out and, although their taste and nutritional values are not adversely affected, they may "feel funny" compared with freeze-dried foods.

MENU PLANNING SHEET   (SAMPLE MENU)

DAY	BREAKFAST	LUNCH	DINNER	SNACKS/NOTES
1	On Road	On Road	Veg. Soup Ham Peas Cookies	Tea Coffee Cocoa Milk

2	Grapefruit Powder
	(or Tang)
	Oatmeal Crunch
	(Granola)
	Sausage Patties, Milk
		Bagels
		Thuringer Sausage
		Fresh Fruit
			Onion Soup
			Chicken a la
			  King w/mashed
			  potatoes
			No bake fruit
			  cobbler
				Tea
				Coffee
				Cocoa
				Milk

3	Prunes Egg with Baco Bits Zweibach	Pilot biscuits Beef Stick Dry Peaches Fruit Drink	Pea Soup Shrimp Creole Hot Mixed Fruit	Tea Coffee Cocoa Milk

4	Orange juice powder
	Apple Pancakes
	Syrup
	Canadian Bacon
		Rye Crisp
		Caraway Seed Cheese
		Raisins
		Fruit drink
			Mushroom Soup
			Freeze Dried
			  Beef Soup
			Jello w/F. D.
			  Strawberries
				Tea
				Coffee
				Cocoa
				Milk

5	Tomato Juice
	Instant Oatmeal
	Cheese Omelette
	Milk
		Wheat Thins
		Beef Sticks
		Apricot Slices
		Fruit Drink
			Chicken Rice
			  Soup
			Taco Comida
			Cabbage/Raisin
			  Salad w/F. D.
			  Cottage cheese or
			  sour cream sauce
				Tea
				Coffee
				Cocoa
				Milk

6	Grape (Welch's) Juice
	Oat Bannock or pan
	Bread
	Meat Balls
		Sesame Crackers
		Swiss Cheese
		Raisins & Nuts
		Fruit Drink
			Tomato Soup
			Beef Strog.
			  w/peas
			No bake cheese
			  cake
				Tea
				Coffee
				Cocoa
				Milk

7	Orange Juice
	Cream of Wheat
	Bacon bar or Western
	  Omelette
		Pilot Biscuits
		Tybo Cheese
		Fruit Drink
			On road or rice
			  Chicken Pilaf
			Peas
			Veg. soup/or
			  Bouillon
				Tea
				Coffee
				Cocoa
				Milk

NOTE: First and last days, usually plan meals on the road. If trip is 2 weeks, repeat
menu but add a special meal for mid-point day. Take advantage of wild berries
on the trail.

DON'T FORGET MARGARINE:
1 tsp. per person for soups,
casseroles, etc.

MENU PLANNING SHEET   (SAMPLE MENU)

DAY	BREAKFAST	LUNCH	DINNER	SNACKS/NOTES

NOTE: First and last days, usually plan meals on the road. If trip is 2 weeks, repeat
menu but add a special meal for mid-point day. Take advantage of wild berries
on the trail.

DON'T FORGET MARGARINE:
1 tsp. per person for soups,
casseroles, etc.

FOOD (MEASURE AND WT. IN GRAMS)			WATER	FOOD ENERGY	PROTEIN	FAT	CARBO
			%	CALORIES		GRAMS	
Apricots (dried)	1 cup	150	25	390	8	1	100
Beans (lima, immature seeds, cooked)	1 cup	170	71	190	13	1	34
Butter	1/2 cup	113	16	810	1	92	1
Cereal (Oatmeal)	1 cup	240	87	130	5	2	23
(Red River)	1/3 cup	56		80			
(Cream o' Wheat)	3/4 cup	168		100	17	2	128
Cheese (Cheddar)	1 oz	28	37	115	7	9	1
(Camembert)	1 wedge	38	52	115	7	9	1
Chicken (canned, boned)	3 oz	85	65	170	18	10	0
Chocolate (sweet)	1 oz	28	1	145	2	9	16
Cocoa (with milk)	1 cup	250	79	245	10	12	27
Corned Beef	3 oz	85	59	185	22	10	0
Corned Beef Hash	3 oz	85	67	155	7	10	9
Corn Oil	1 tbsp	14	0	125	0	14	0
Dandelion Greens (cooked)	1 cup	180	90	60	4	1	12
Dates (pitted, cut)	1 cup	178	22	490	4	1	130
Figs (dried, large)	1 fig	21	23	60	1		15
Honey	1 tbsp	21	17	65		0	17
Macaroni (cooked)	1 cup	140	72	155	5	1	32
Milk (dry, skim)	1 cup	68	4	245	24		35
Peanuts (roasted, shelled halves)	1 cup	144	2	840	37	72	27
Peanut Butter	1 tbsp	16	2	95	4	8	3
Peas (green, whole dried)	1 cup	250	70	290	20	1	52
Pilot Bread	(1 biscuit)	15	30	100	2	5	13
Potato (boiled in peel)	1	136	80	105	3		23
Prunes (raw)	4	32	28	70	1		18

Raisins (Muscat, seeded)	1 cup	165	18	480	4		128
Rice (white) enriched instant	1 cup	165	73	180	4		40
Rye-Krisp	1 wafer	13	6	45	2		10
Sardines	3 oz	85	62	175	20	9	0
Shrimp (canned, meat)	3 oz	85	70	100	21	1	1
Spaghetti	1 cup	140	72	155	5	1	32
Sugar (white, granulated)	1 cup	200		770	0	0	199
Tuna (canned in oil, drained solids)	3 oz	85	61	170	24	7	0
Wholewheat Bread	(1 slice)	28	36	65	3	1	14

the evening has been the dominant image of wilderness travel.

However, the evidence is almost overwhelming in favor of campfire bans or strong encouragement to avoid them. Foresters speak of the "human browse line" which moves higher and higher on standing trees and farther and farther away from regular campsites as time passes. This browse line is the limits campers go to in order to have firewood. They break off dead branches from standing trees,

forage farther and farther from the campsite for fallen trees and branches, and worst of all, begin chopping down living trees for firewood. Soon the forest resembles a pruned and clean-swept orchard with only trees and barren ground beneath them, leaving nothing to decompose as part of the normal course of events in forests.

While there are great wilder-nesses remaining, particularly in Canada and Alaska—where campfires leave no permanent damage if built

A pit fire is shown with the sod carefully removed so it can be replaced when the fire is out.

Another solution to preventing fires from spreading underground is to use a large flat rock with soil on top of it to prevent blackening the rock.

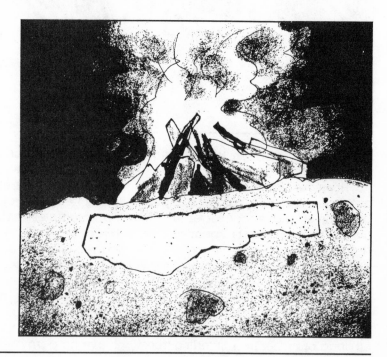

properly—the improper use of campfires presents a problem even in some of those remote areas.

Still, it is possible to build campfires in some places. You should check with the land-managing agency before trips to be certain fires are permissible and to learn what restrictions are imposed.

With all this background, it is no surprise that everyone you talk to about backpacking and virtually everything you read on the subject will tell you always to take a packstove and plenty of fuel. There are a number of good arguments in favor of using packstoves for cooking instead of wood fires. Stoves give you more control over cooking; they don't blacken your pots and pans; they leave absolutely no evidence they were ever there; and they do not cause fires by flying sparks on tents, clothing, or sleeping bags.

However, if you do build a campfire, there are several things you should remember:

- All fires must be attended.
- Be aware of overuse. If your firepit is full of wood ash or the surrounding area trampled flat, clean the campsite to lessen the scars.
- Fires should be built away from tents, trees, overhanging branches, underground root systems—and away from large rocks, so they won't be permanently stained.
- They should never be built on top of the forest floor. Ground covers of needles or decomposed matter should be cleared away, then replaced when the fire is out.
- If the wind is blowing, do not build a fire because of the danger of flying sparks that could start a forest fire.
- Fires should not be ringed with rocks

because it blackens them. Instead, use one of the following methods of insuring little or no impact on the forest floor:

The flat rock method: Spread bare soil on top of a flat rock and build the fire on the soil. Be sure all wood is completely burned; when the fire is out, crush the ash into the soil and remove everything from the rock, washing it away with water, leaving no trace of the fire.

The pit method: Remove topsoil or sod in large chunks from an area about 12" by 24", or even smaller, and remove all burnable material from the area around the pit. Keep the topsoil or sod together in a neat pile. When breaking camp, be sure the bottom and sides of the firepit are cold to the touch, then crush all coals to powder or paste and mix with the clean soil before replacing the soil and sod. Tramp down the covered firepit to be sure no soft spots exist that will sink later and cause a mud puddle.

BACKPACKER'S TIP

If you are traveling with only one companion, a good way to heat water for soups and hot drinks is to use an aluminum beverage can with the top cut out. It is thermally more efficient because of its shape; it holds heat longer than larger or flatter containers; and as the water heats, it rises to the top so you can pour off the top half for the first drink or cup of soup, then refill it and have the start of another cup of hot water.

The surface method: When you have an abundance of bare soil, there is no need to disturb the topsoil by digging a firepit. Spread several inches of bare soil on the ground and build a fire on it. When you are breaking camp, be sure all wood is burned, crush the coals and ashes, mix them with soil and spread them around the area.

FIREWOOD

As noted earlier, natural firewood (fallen timber and branches) is becoming more and more scarce. Indeed, it is virtually nonexistent in popular desert camping areas. When you do find firewood in an area where wood fires are permitted, use only what is necessary and keep your fires small.

Do not break off branches, either alive or dead, from standing trees because a forest with stubs instead of branches loses much of its aesthetic appeal.

Leave saws and axes at home and use only firewood you can break by hand. They also lighten your load when left at home.

EXTINGUISHING FIRES

Mix water and soil with the coals and ash of the fire, and feel the coals with your bare hands to be sure they are dead. Then scatter or bury the ashes. Also scatter any unused firewood to help preserve a natural appearance in the area.

CHAPTER 15

THE WEATHER

Mankind is endlessly fascinated with weather. It is one of those things that exerts enormous control over our lives, but over which in return, we exert virtually no control. Even with attempts to create rain, we still cannot cause rain to fall unless conditions are just right. So we talk about the weather, listen to it discussed on television for hours each day, and try to learn how to live with it.

Backpacking is one sport that is very dependent on the weather, even though many backpackers plan trips without even considering the weather. If it rains, so be it, they say and go ahead about the business of tramping through the wilderness with a system of layered clothing to be prepared for both wet and dry.

But subconsciously, many backpackers become almost as accurate at predicting weather as the television weatherpersons with their satellite photos and wire-service information.

Weather plays a major role in every backpacking trip you take, whether it be monotonously fair and calm, or cold, dark and blustery. Few scenes are more dramatic than watching a thunderstorm come sweeping across the plains toward you, especially if you have your shelter established and can watch it without racing for cover. By the same token, many backpackers in the mountains remember vividly the time a late-spring snowstorm caught them above timberline and how they had to set up a hasty camp to sit it out, and woke

the next morning with several inches of snow outside the tent.

And nobody will ever forget getting caught on a high, barren ridge with an electrical storm coming in and smelling ozone in the air and hearing electricity snapping on their backpacks and feeling their hair being forced to stand on end by the electrical charges in the air. Most, fortunately, have lived to tell of it, but some have not because they didn't take the proper precautions against being struck by lightning.

The weather creates many ironies in traveling in the wilderness. You may be hiking a remote stretch of coastline and run out of fresh water because no streams empty into the ocean. Some beach hikers have had to stop for several hours to build solar stills to get fresh water. When you are hiking in a rainstorm in warm weather, sometimes it seems more reasonable to forget about raingear entirely because it is so hot and suffocating that your clothing and body become drenched with sweat anyway. Clearly, weather

is a problem with no final solutions. We simply learn how to live with it.

But there are some measures we can take to give us a very general idea of what is going on in the atmosphere. One way to do this is learn the various clouds and cloud formations and the general trends in weather they indicate. This is never an entirely accurate method, but it can at least limit the number of unpleasant surprises you will receive.

Here are some of the old-fashioned bad weather indicators that are reasonably accurate. But only reasonably:

- A ring around the sun or moon means rain or snow.
- Windshifts from north to west and then south are often followed by rain.
- Unusual sky colors, such as green, yellow, dark red, or slate-blue, bring rain or wind or both.
- Small black clouds bring rain.
- Unless clouds that hang high overhead lift by midday, they usually bring wind and rain.

- Scud clouds, those which are small, black, and moving fast beneath a dark stratus layer, tell of the approach of rain and wind. If you can see them above the stratus, they usually mean there will be wind only.
- Cloud layers moving in different directions indicate a change in wind direction to that of the upper layer's direction.

Fair weather indicators:

- A gray dawn means good weather.
- Fog lying low in valleys will usually burn off and the day will be clear.
- Rain rarely falls after dew forms.

- Cumulus clouds on sunny days indicate fair weather, unless they form into tall shapes with flattened tops.
- Red sky at morning, shepherd's warning. Red sky at night, sailor's delight.

Without attempting to write an introductory course on weather characteristics and predictions, suffice it to say that the basic concern of everyone who works or plays outdoors is what has become known as "fronts". Reduced to their basic definition, a front is where two differing air masses meet. One air mass may be stable, dry, and calm, while the other is wet, moving,

Cumulonimbus

Cumulus

Fractocumulus

Cirrocumulus

Altocumulus

Cirrostratus

Altostratus

Nimbostratus

Cirrus

Stratus

Stratocumulus

and with violent tendencies. Where these two meet is the front; and the unstable, violent mass usually pushes against the other creating what we commonly call weather—meaning rain, snow, thunderstorms, and the like.

Fronts are generally either warm or cold, which refers to the differences between the air masses and between temperatures on the ground and in the air.

A cold front is often unstable and the resulting weather is usually violent, although cold fronts usually don't last as long as warm fronts. Most cold fronts (remember, where the two air masses meet) usually travel at a speed between 20 and 35 miles per hour and may be preceded by a line of thunderstorms from 50 to 200 miles ahead of it.

A warm front is usually more stable, moist and has lower clouds and limited visibility. These fronts move more slowly than cold fronts and the rain they bring may fall for several days. Their arrival is more easily predicted by a drop in barometric pressure and a predictable sequence of clouds.

CLOUDS

Clouds may be best defined as evidence of moisture content in the air. They also tell you other things, such as wind speed, general atmospheric conditions, and what to expect in a few minutes, or hours, or days.

They are divided into three different families:

- **Cirrus**: these are high, thin, and wispy.
- **Cumulus**: billowy like big cushions

or soapsuds, and because they're always moving, favorites for children of all ages to imagine what they see in them.
- **Stratus**: these are layered in horizontal bands at very high altitudes.

What does this mean for you when you're trying to predict the weather? Other than a normal amount of confusion over their identification so you can impress your companions with your meteorological knowledge, they can also tell you something about present and future conditions. But first you must learn some of the sub-species of each cloud, because they have a knack of intermingling and becoming a little of each.

For example, very high fluffy clouds may be cirrocumulus and equally high but thin clouds may be cirrostratus. And a more flat layer can be stratocumulus.

Of more practical value are the clouds preceded by the word "alto." "Alto" means the clouds are in the middle elevation range below the cirrus group and above the stratus.

"Nimbus" clouds are rain-bearing, and the term is used with the cumulus and stratus families, hence cumulonimbus and nimbostratus.

A third term is "fracto," meaning broken or ragged on the underside, also meaning it is raining or snowing or hailing from them.

Back to the basics, here is what the more common ones usually mean:

Cirrus: These are often the leading edge of a warm front as the warm air rides over the colder mass it meets. The clouds are actually ice crystals and often indicate a change of weather within two or three days. These also may be the first clouds to appear in an otherwise clear sky.

Cirrocumulus: These are high, wavy groups of clouds and are sometimes called "mackerel sky." They often form in windrows like hay ready for the bailer or waves painted by an amateur seascape artist. A good indicator of violent weather behind it.

Cirrostratus: High, white, thin sheets of clouds that do not block the sun or moon, but may form a yellowish-halo around the sun or moon.

Altocumulus: These are often confused with cirrocumulus, but the wavy rows are composed of larger clouds than these in the cirro group. May create a sun or moon corona, a disc of color around the light source as the light shines through water instead of the cirro ice. The corona will have several colors in it instead of the yellowish cirro halo.

Stratocumulus: These are flattened masses of cumulus clouds that are not usually rain clouds, although they can regroup to form nimbostratus, which is a rain cloud.

Altostratus: A middle-height gray layer of clouds that blocks the sun and moon but has thin spots through which they may show. These are usually rain clouds with a drizzle instead of downpour.

Stratus: A low, gray mass that produces only a drizzle. May hang overhead for days at a time.

Nimbostratus: The classic rain cloud that is thick, low and composed of layers. While rain is falling in a distance you can see the fracto, or ragged, underside. When it is falling on you, this isn't so obvious.

Cumulus: These are fair-weather clouds that usually form on pleasant afternoons when the sun heats the earth and forces moisture upward. Most cumulus clouds dissipate in the evening as the moisture descends again, usually in the form of dew.

Cumulonimbus: Thunderheads. These are the dark, billowing masses with flat tops that produce thunder, rain, hail, snow flurries, and so forth.

HOW TO SEE A FRONT COMING

A cold front is almost always preceded by altostratus that is then followed by nimbostratus, and sometimes cumulostratus. The barometer will drop steadily, meaning your altimeter will rise, the temperature will drop and the winds will usually come from the north or northwest, then shift to the south or southwest. If you carry a barometer or altimeter, you will know the front has passed when the instruments reverse themselves; the barometer will rise and altimeter will fall. Clearing will come when the stratocumulus bands begin forming, followed by altocumulus and finally clearing, provided, of course, that another front isn't directly behind.

A warm front is usually foretold by a series of cloud sequences. Cirrus will be seen about 48 hours ahead of the front, followed by cirrostratus, then altostratus, and finally nimbostratus.

The barometer will drop, altimeters will rise slowly. The temperature will rise and your visibility will be hampered by haze, fog, and lowered cloud cover. Winds will be minimal, if present at all. Rains come and often stay even while the barometer is rising and altimeter falling, and the clearing process may take as long as two or three days after the front passes.

To insulate yourself from lightning that might travel through the damp ground, unroll your sleeping pad, place your pack on the pad, then sit on the pack. Also stay away from trees and stay low until the storm passes.

LIGHTNING

Lightning storms are one of the most beautiful events you can witness in the wilderness, particularly if you have a good view of the proceedings and are in a safe place. In spite of its obvious dangers, very, very few people are struck by lightning. This is partly luck because lightning strikes the point on the ground closest to the cloud overhead from which it comes. Except for people on exposed ridges or in open fields, a person is usually much smaller than trees, buildings, boulders, and other objects outdoors.

However, you should know how to avoid becoming a convenient target for a strike before you go outdoors or are caught there during an electrical storm.

The dangers of lightning are being hit by a direct strike, by ground currents that are carried from the point of the strike through the ground to you, or by currents which pass through the air from the strike to you.

Lightning goes from the clouds to the earth in the shortest possible distance and along the path of least resistance. Veterans of mountaineering tell of incidents when the air around them ionized as it became charged with electricity. During such times an object that is a conductor, such as an ice axe or packframe, gives off a crackling noise as small sparks fly. Sometimes a blue glow know as St. Elmo's Fire can be seen. If a person is the conductor, his or her hair will stand on end and crackle—a distinctly unpleasant sensation.

This does not always mean that the person or object is going to be struck by lightning; otherwise, everyone to whom it has happened would have been a target. But it does mean that you should take immediate action, such as getting yourself away from the exposed ridge, getting rid of the pack, and lying low until the storm passes.

Following are general safety rules for avoiding being struck by lightning:

- Avoid all moist areas, such as gullies and crevices, because moisture is a conductor of electricity.
- When sitting, occupy as little space as possible. Keep your hands off the ground and your feet together so you won't span a large distance in case of ground currents.
- Sit or crouch on insulating objects, such as a coil of rope or a dry sleeping bag.

- Avoid depressions in the ground. It is better to be a bit higher than the lowest point, but at not the highest point, of course.
- Avoid overhangs and small caves. A large cave might be safe, provided it isn't the terminus of a damp crevice in the rockface.
- When on a ledge, crouch at the outer edge away from the wall to avoid ground current. But tie yourself to the ledge, if possible, in case you are thrown off by a shock wave.
- Dry synthetic rope is the best insulator.

The possibility of you or a companion being struck by lightning, as noted earlier, is very remote. Some people have been struck directly by lightning and survived, and others have suffered severe burns where the current entered or left their body. The two major injuries caused by lightning are cardiac arrest from the electrical shock and burns. In the case of cardiac arrest, you should perform mouth-to-mouth resuscitation immediately, and treat burns as explained elsewhere in the first-aid chapter.

CHAPTER 16

FIRST AID

One of the most fascinating aspects of the Lewis and Clark Expedition of 1804–06—perhaps the greatest adventure in backpacking in American history—is the medical problems faced during the two-year trip and the methods of treating sickness and injury. Only one man was lost, apparently from a ruptured appendix, and he would have died anyway because the first successful appendectomy wasn't accomplished for several years after the expedition.

A brief reading of the medical matters in the explorers' journals is the list of equipment taken along and how it was used to treat the men. Captain Meriwether Lewis was trained in medicine by the best doctors in Philadelphia and Washington, D.C., and it was a good thing: he treated men for boils, absesses, sore feet, sunstroke, fever, headaches, colic, snakebites, and rheumatism, among other ailments.

One of the most popular forms of treatment then was draining blood from the body. While Sacajawea was in labor giving birth to "Little Pomp," she was given pieces of rattlesnake rattle to eat and speed the delivery. Mercury ointment was given for stomachaches; calomel and jalap were administered for the same purpose. Opium was prescribed for most pains.

Fortunately, medical knowledge has improved somewhat since the early 19th century, and the cures that can easily kill have been erased from first-aid manuals and survival instructions. Interestingly, one of the most recent changes adopted was the treatment of frostbite. Until only the past decade or two, this injury was treated by rubbing snow on the damaged skin or immersion in cold water. Both treatments actually increased the damage. Now the injured area is heated to stop the damage and increase the flow of blood, which begins the healing process. And the damaged area is not rubbed, as in the past, to restore circulation because that, too, only increases the damage.

Since most backpackers are in good health and good physical condition—and all but rank beginners are aware of the most common dangers—the majority of medical mishaps on backpacking trips are minor injuries that can be treated quickly and easily within a few minutes, and the party is soon back on the trail. These injuries are the cuts, minor burns, bruises, and abrasions that can happen anywhere: someone picks up a pot thinking it is cool, and isn't; or a finger is pinched while putting up or taking down the tent.

But there are always the unexpected emergencies and sudden illnesses that strike anywhere—while working in the yard, sitting at the office desk, or driving home from work. These illnesses and accidents each require basic first-aid knowledge. And unless you backpack with the family doctor, you will have to learn the basics of first aid before heading for the back country.

You can learn basic first aid in classes offered by several organizations. The best remains those offered by the American Red Cross through your employer, at local YMCAs and YWCAs, and by other quasi-public organizations. Many outdoor clubs offer

classes several times a year, and for backpacking and other forms of outdoor recreation, these are perhaps the best since they deal with such matters as the best way to evacuate the injured or ill from deep in the wilderness.

Each backpacking party should have at least one fully equipped first-aid kit; and if there is a chance the group may split into two or more smaller groups for day hikes, then a completely stocked first-aid kit should be taken along by each group. You can make up these kits yourself or buy those already packed in convenient boxes from many outdoor recreation suppliers.

If you travel in areas where poisonous snakes are common, you should carry a snake-bite kit and be certain you know exactly how to use it. Most kits are equipped with a small knife for lacerating the bitten area and a small suction device for removing as much of the venom as possible.

Be sure you check with your family physician or your city, county, state, or federal health authorities for recommendations on what the kit should include, especially what kind of antivenin you should carry. Not every medical researcher agrees on the use of antivenin by anyone other than qualified medical people, so do some research on this matter before traveling in snake country. It is safest to call the hospital nearest the area in which you'll be backpacking before you leave on the trip. If they decline to make recommendations, they can refer you to a local medical information source.

Although you should always carry a first-aid manual, and have its instructions virtually memorized before you leave on backpacking trips, here

are a few of the most common ailments or injuries related to outdoor activities.

Burns: In the case of minor burns—a finger slips and hits a hot grill or bacon fat—immerse the burned area in cold water immediately, then gently wash the area with a liquid soap, using sterile cotton soaked in sterile water. Boiled water that has been cooled is best.

Then cover the burn with a layer of sterile dressing coated with petroleum jelly or a similar salve to keep the burned area from sticking to the cotton dressing. Then cover this with a larger and thicker bandage with only enough pressure against the skin to keep it in place. This dressing is only to avoid the possibility of infection.

If a burn is much larger and covers a wide area of skin, take the victim to a doctor as soon as possible. Keep the burned area free of all clothing, jewelry, and other foreign objects. Keep the burned area as immobile as possible to avoid further tissue damage.

Heat exhaustion and sunstroke: The best treatment is to take preventive measures before heat exhaustion and sunstroke happen. Be sure everyone in your party has an adequate salt intake and drinks sufficient fluids.

Heat exhaustion is caused by prolonged physical activity in a hot climate and occurs when the blood vessels in the skin become so dilated that they rob the supply of blood to the brain and other vital organs. The result is fainting; heat exhaustion usually isn't particularly serious. Instead, it is a warning to stop the activity and take preventive measures, such as seeking shade and rest, salt, and liquids. Other indicators include rapid heartbeat and a headache.

Heatstroke (often called sunstroke) is almost the exact opposite of hypothermia (see later in this chapter) and can be fatal if not treated quickly and properly. The victim's body must be cooled as rapidly as possible, either by immersion in tepid (not cold) water, the application of wet towels or blankets over the entire body, or towels soaked in alcohol, if it is available.

This condition can occur rapidly. The victim will seem normal and suddenly become confused, irrational, and uncoordinated. The body temperature shoots up to 105° F or even higher, with no sweating.

Rapid treatment must be emphasized. The cooling process must begin immediately. When the body temperature is brought down, the victim will gradually regain a sense of bearings and become rational again, but the recovery can take several days with the temperature fluctuating up and down. Obviously, the victim must be evacuated for medical care as soon as possible.

Stretcher cases: Sometimes an injured backpacker can walk out using a makeshift crutch, or by leaning on a companion. But in the case of broken legs, severe sprains, or serious internal injuries, a stretcher may be the only possible means of evacuating the victim.

You will have to fashion one from whatever materials you have on hand. The simplest and easiest to make is to use slender saplings, forming the sling by slipping the poles through the sleeves of parkas. Two sturdy parkas will usually support the victim.

Others can be fashioned of packframes, although it is a bit trickier.

But if the injury is especially serious, a head wound, or spinal injury, it is best to send the strongest hiker out for help while the other members of the group stay with the injured hiker. Helicopter rescues are usually expensive, but they are both faster and safer than attempting to carry the victim out to the trailhead.

Shock: This is often as dangerous as the injury itself, and each serious injury should be treated with this in mind. Shock is caused by a sudden reduction in the volume of blood flowing through the victim's system. This reduction is due to a defense mechanism that causes the rush of blood serum to the injured area to start the healing process immediately. Consequently, the arteries constrict and divert the blood supply to the vital organs, and the heart begins pumping faster to circulate the blood and to help in the healing process.

The symptoms are easy to spot. The victim becomes pale. The skin becomes cool to the touch, first the extremities and later the torso. As the shock deepens, the victim becomes sweaty, yet cold to the touch, and soon is dehydrated. The pulse may be rapid, and breathing fast and shallow, while the blood pressure drops.

It is best to treat the causes of the shock first, such as severe bleeding. In the case of burns, it is the loss of body fluids that causes it, so the victim should be fed liquids to replace those lost.

Place the victim flat on the ground, then elevate the feet at least twelve inches above the level of the head. Hot water bottles, heated stones, and body-to-body contact will help raise the body temperature. Keep the victim prone and warm, and encourage drinking warm liquids until the victim is stable. Then evacuate the victim as soon as possible.

Broken bones: Fractures are usu-

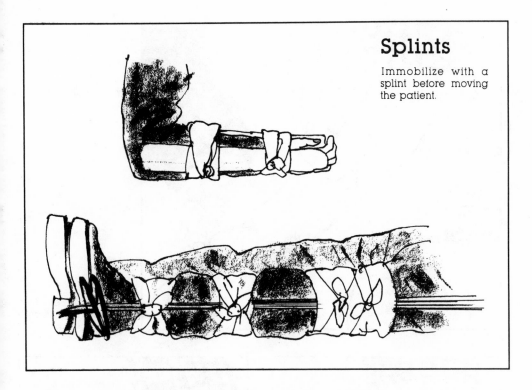

Splints

Immobilize with a splint before moving the patient.

ally easy to diagnose if the fracture is compound: the bone may well protrude from the skin. In simple fractures, discoloration and swelling will soon set in, and the area will be painful to the touch. Sometimes a simple fracture is easily confused with a bad sprain, especially in joints such as the ankle. But the first-aid treatment is the same in either case.

The victim should lie down while you make a splint to cover the injured area to prevent further damage. Do not make an attempt to set the broken bone; that is a job for doctors only. Your main concern will be making a splint to keep the injured area immobilized.

For a splint to function properly, the splints must anchor the limb both above and below the break or sprain. Pad the splint so it won't rub against the skin.

It is possible, but certainly not desirable, for the victim to move the injured leg if the break is below the knee. But if it is above, the victim should be immobilized and carried out.

Arm and shoulder sprains or fractures should also be immobilized and a sling fashioned to keep the arm tied against the chest.

Severe cuts: Rather than recommending the memorization of all the pressure points throughout the body where arteries can be pressed to restrict the blood flow, most medical people now recommend simply applying pressure to the wound itself to stop the blood flow. Tourniquets have also fallen into disfavor because few people know how to use them properly; they can cause as much damage by restricting the blood flow than they can solve.

So in the case of severe bleeding,

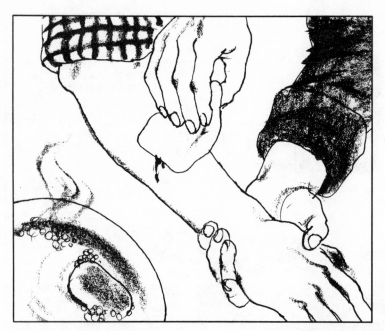

Use your first-aid kit to cleanse and bandage the wound.

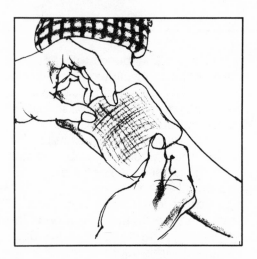

apply the pressure directly against the wound and hold a sterile bandage against the wound to help clotting occur. You can do this by hand at first, then when initial clotting has occurred, wrap the wound tightly with a battle dressing and keep the victim immobile until you are certain solid clotting has occurred. Then keep the victim as immobile as possible until medical assistance can be obtained.

When wrapping this bandage, be sure you don't shut off all the blood below the wound. If the skin begins to turn dark, or if the victim complains of numbness, the bandage is too tight.

Insect bites and poisonous plants: For mosquito, no-seeum, chig-

TICKS

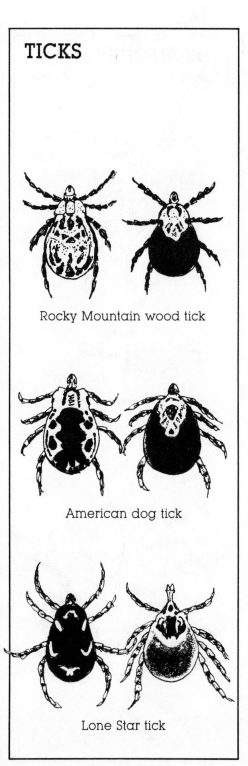

Rocky Mountain wood tick

American dog tick

Lone Star tick

ger, and similar insect bites, and for poison oak, poison ivy and poison sumac irritations, the relatively new cortisone-based creams available over the counter are the best medicines. Calamine lotion also helps relieve the itching.

If, in the case of poison plants, the rash spreads over a large area, you can make a solution of saltwater (2 teaspoons per quart) and apply a compress several times a day.

Bee and hornet stings: Do not attempt to remove the stinger with tweezers. Make a paste of soda and water, then coat the stung area. Some people become allergic to bee stings

---

BACKPACKER'S TIP

An excellent relief for insect bites are the relatively new cortisone creams now available without prescription.

---

and can go into shock. In this case, antihistamine tablets should be taken.

Spiders: Only two types of spiders present any problem to people backpacking in North America: the black widow and brown, or recluse, spiders. Their bites are seldom fatal, and then usually to the weak and elderly or to infants. But the bites are painful to everyone. Antivenin is available, but is administered only by doctors.

The black widow bite causes severe pain, often muscle spasms and abdominal pain. These usually go away in two to four days, but weakness may last a week or longer.

The brown spider bite causes inflammation around the bitten area, followed by a blister that eventually ruptures leaving the area discolored.

Ticks: These bloodsucking parasites live mainly in hardwood forests and around open ranges where cattle graze. They seldom are found in high elevations above timberline or in cool, damp climates.

You should check your body at least once each day for ticks because you won't always feel them when they sink their teeth into your skin. Check around your boot tops, beltline, armpits, crotch, and any folds in your skin where they can find protection.

Remove ticks by applying heat to them, such as a hot stick end or a piece of metal heated over the stove. Or you can first try a dab of alcohol or stove fuel. Sometimes they can simply be pulled off, but the danger in doing so is leaving the head still imbedded in your skin. If you do leave an imbedded head, sterilize a sharp knife, make a small incision, and remove the head. Then swab the area with antiseptic.

BACKPACKER'S TIP

It is best to keep your first-aid kit in its own compartment on your pack rather than scattered through several pockets or even in several different packs. Many of the top-line packs have leather accessory patches built onto them for the fanny packs. If not, you can sew them on yourself. But the first-aid kit should be easy to detach—and always be fully stocked.

POISONOUS PLANTS

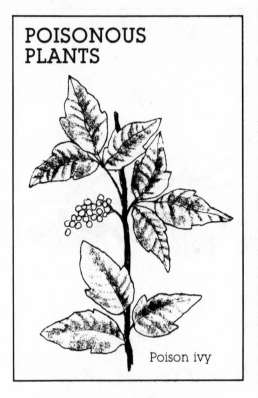

Poison ivy

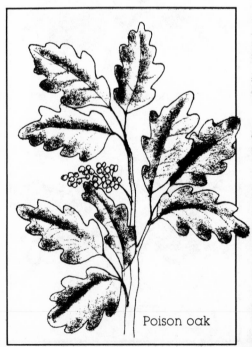

Poison oak

Poison sumac

Lost: The person who is lost has only one basic thing to worry about: staying alive. If anyone knows you are out and didn't return when expected, a search party will come. Making a shelter is the first priority. A shallow cave, fallen timber, and boulders will serve the purpose.

High ground is better than low because a cold fog may settle into hollows and valleys. Insulate your shelter with brush, leaves, and grass to protect you against the cold ground.

Keep warm, dry, and insulated.

The best signal is a fire, made with green wood to create heavy smoke. But don't add to your problems by starting a forest fire.

HYPOTHERMIA

For decades, if not centuries, this condition—which has been the greatest danger to those working or playing outdoors—was called simply exposure. Occasionally you will still see references in newspapers to a lost hiker or hunter who suffered from exposure when found. During the past several years, the condition has been more accurately described as hypothermia, from the Greek: **hypo** meaning "under" or "below," and **thermia** or **thermes** meaning "heat."

Put simply, it describes the condition when the body core temperature falls below the normal 98.6° F.

Because the condition has received so much publicity and research funding (including studies sponsored by the Eddie Bauer Co.), fewer and fewer people fall victim to it each year. The massive education program supported by nearly every outdoor organization and equipment supplier in North America has paid off.

But it is still a condition which outdoorspeople must constantly guard against; they must be able to recognize its symptoms when they occur.

Hypothermia occurs when the body heat is lost faster than the body can replace it. When the body temperature drops more than three degrees below the 98.6° F., certain changes occur in the body and mind. Prevention is reasonably simple; dress properly and be prepared for sudden changes in the weather. Body heat loss can occur in the middle of summer, just as it is a constant situation to guard against during the cooler months. A day hike to the top of a high ridge with the group wearing only tee-shirts and jeans can suddenly change into a desperate situation should a rain come up, or simply a hard, cold wind begin to blow.

HYPOTHERMIA

Hypothermia victims go through four stages of the condition unless treated promptly and properly.

Shivering

Uncontrolled, violent shivering, and difficulty with speech

Erratic movements, stiff muscles, and inability to think clearly

Irrational behavior, unconsciousness, and death

It is essential to treat the hypothermia victim quickly.

Get the victim warm and into dry clothing.

Stoke up a big fire.

Feed the victim hot drinks.

Walk the victim around to force his or her body to rebuild its own heat sources.

Once the danger is past, keep the victim warm and comfortable.

Obviously, the prevention for this is to be certain the whole group is wearing or carrying sufficiently warm clothing for such an event. Sometimes a wool shirt will be sufficient, but a wind shell or a water-repellent parka is much better. Nearly all jeans have a high cotton content, and cotton is virtually worthless as an insulator. So when backpackers obey the rules of always carrying the Ten Essentials, the danger is virtually eliminated.

Hypothermia is easy to diagnose for both the victim and companions, although some victims are reluctant to admit that they may be in trouble. So use the buddy system, in the event bad weather catches you unprepared.

The condition is broken down into several stages, the first of which is shivering—the warning sign that sends most people in search of shelter or warmer clothing. Shivering, then, is the first signal and should be heeded.

Unless checked, the next stage is violent, uncontrollable shivering, the kind that can make your teeth chatter and cause difficulty in speaking.

Following this, sometimes almost immediately, the shivering decreases and muscles become stiff. You will make erratic movements and won't be able to think clearly. If allowed to continue without treatment, the next stage is irrationality and stupor, followed by unconsciousness and, finally, by death.

Hypothermia affects each person differently. One backpacker may be shivering in misery, while a companion is only mildly chilly and otherwise unaffected. Too many outdoors people associate getting cold easily with being soft or out of condition. While there may be some truth to the latter belief in some cases, that is beside the

EMERGENCY PROCEDURES

Since most of us react more swiftly by following established procedures, or through a system we can understand, the Red Cross and various search-and-rescue organizations have created step-by-step methods of dealing with emergencies.

One such system is called the Seven Steps:

1. In any emergency, someone must take charge. Immediately.

2. Approach the victim safely. Some injured climbers and hikers have had their injuries compounded by anxious companions who dislodged rocks on the way down to help them.

3. Always treat for shock.

4. Perform urgently needed first aid first. Lack of breathing or pulse are the paramount concerns. Treat other injuries next.

5. Check for other injuries after obvious ones have been treated.

6. Plan what to do. Be quick and cool. Whether to leave the victim right there, or to attempt to evacuate. Who should be sent for help and who should stay.

7. Carry out the plan. Get everyone in the group helping because busy hands are more likely to clear minds of panic. If the victim is to remain while someone goes for help, it is the

job of others to build shelters and prepare meals.

Another approach is called the ABCs (with an occasional letter of the alphabet missing):

Airway management: Learn artificial respiration and mouth-to-mouth resuscitation, and use it until the victim can breathe independently.

Bleeding: Severe bleeding must be treated immediately. Loss of blood needs quick action, and direct pressure on the wound will at least slow most bleeding.

Choking: Two methods of dislodging whatever is choking a person can be used. Each system has its own adherents, and either is usually effective.

1. From behind wrap your arms around the victim's waist. Make a fist and place the thumb against the victim's abdomen, slightly above the navel and below the rib cage. Grasp your fist with your other hand and press into the abdomen with a quick upward thrust. Repeat until the foreign matter is dislodged.

2. Bend the victim over with head between knees and give four vigorous back blows between the shoulders.

And still another version is to use what is called the "finder sweep," probing the victim's mouth and throat if the foreign matter is high in the throat.

point. Physiological differences determine each person's immunity to cold, just as it determines individual heat or pain thresholds.

When one or more members of your group begins shivering violently (and probably suffering in silence), act quickly. Get them into dry and warm clothing and under some kind of shelter. Feed them hot drinks and high-energy foods, such as chocolate and raisins. Hot chocolate is an excellent antidote. When they are dry, put them into a warm sleeping bag, or if it isn't raining, force them to walk and jump and do exercises while keeping high-energy food available. Help the body rebuild its own resources in this manner.

If it is simply too cold and wet outside, get them into shelter and warm. Build a fire and move them as close to it as possible (you will probably be forgiven breaking bans on campfires if they are built for this purpose).

Heat rocks and wrap them in cloth or articles of clothing and insert them into the bag with the victim. Strip all the victim's clothes off and your own and slip into the sleeping bag with the victim. If the bag is large enough and no other source of heat is available, put two warm persons in the bag with the victim, making the victim a sandwich between two warm bodies.

It is essential to work quickly.

Do not feed the victim alcoholic drinks because alcohol is a depressant rather than a stimulant, and it can only increase the problem.

By taking these measures, you quickly turn a potentially dangerous situation into a temporary situation that anyone can easily handle. But always take quick action, so it will be only a mild problem.

Wind Chill Chart

WIND SPEED MPH	COOLING POWER OF WIND EXPRESSED AS "EQUIVALENT CHILL TEMPERATURE"																				
	TEMPERATURE (°F)																				
CALM	40	35	30	25	20	15	10	5	0	-5	-10	-15	-20	-25	-30	-35	-40	-45	-50	-55	-60
	EQUIVALENT CHILL TEMPERATURE																				
5	35	30	25	20	15	10	5	0	-5	-10	-15	-20	-25	-30	-35	-40	-45	-50	-55	-65	-70
10	30	20	15	10	5	0	-10	-15	-20	-25	-35	-40	-45	-50	-60	-65	-70	-75	-80	-90	-95
15	25	15	10	0	-5	-10	-20	-25	-30	-40	-45	-50	-60	-65	-70	-80	-85	-90	-100	-105	-110
20	20	10	5	0	-10	-15	-25	-30	-35	-45	-50	-60	-65	-75	-80	-85	-95	-100	-110	-115	-120
25	15	10	0	-5	-15	-20	-30	-35	-45	-50	-60	-65	-75	-80	-90	-95	-105	-110	-120	-125	-135
30	10	5	0	-10	-20	-25	-30	-40	-50	-55	-65	-70	-80	-85	-95	-100	-110	-115	-125	-130	-140
35	10	5	-5	-10	-20	-30	-35	-40	-50	-60	-65	-75	-80	-90	-100	-105	-115	-120	-130	-135	-145
40	10	0	-5	-15	-20	-30	-35	-45	-55	-60	-70	-75	-85	-95	-100	-110	-115	-125	-130	-140	-150

WINDS ABOVE 40 HAVE LITTLE ADDITIONAL EFFECT.

LITTLE DANGER   INCREASING DANGER (Flesh may freeze within 1 min.)   GREAT DANGER (Flesh may freeze within 30 seconds)

DANGER OF FREEZING EXPOSED FLESH FOR PROPERLY CLOTHED PERSONS

Source: National Weather Service, U.S. Dept. of Commerce

Summer* Weather Chart

Regions	Normal Monthly Precip. (in.)	Normal Daily Max. Temp.	Normal Daily Min. Temp.	Normal Daily Mean Temp.	Average % of Poss. Sunshine
Pacific N.W.					
Seattle	1.08	73.8	53.7	63.8	62
Spokane	.58	81.9	54.0	68.0	77
California					
Bay Area	.03	71.6	54.3	63.0	65
Los Angeles	.02	75.8	63.2	69.5	83
Interior	.05	91.3	56.9	74.1	96
Colorado					
Denver	1.29	85.8	57.4	71.6	72
MN/WI					
Minneapolis/ St. Paul	3.05	80.8	59.6	70.2	67
IL/MI					
Chicago	2.73	82.3	59.9	71.1	68
Detroit	3.04	81.6	62.1	71.9	65
N. Atlantic States					
Boston	3.46	79.3	63.3	71.3	67
Mid-Atlantic States					
Wash. D.C.	4.67	86.6	67.6	77.1	63

*Figures are for August, normally the warmest, sunniest month. Source: U.S. National Oceanic and Atmospheric Administration, as reported in "Statistical Abstract of the United States," U.S. Dept. of Commerce, Bureau of the Census. Temperatures recorded at airports, in Fahrenheit degrees.

A BASIC FIRST-AID KIT

ITEM	QUANTITY AND SIZE	USE	ITEM	QUANTITY AND SIZE	USE
Accident form & Pencil*	Two	To ensure accurate informaion is communicated to rescue assistance	Roller gauze*	2 rolls 2" × 5 yds.	For holding gauze flats in place
Aspirin*	12 tablets —5 grain	1 to 2 every four hours for pain	Safety pins	Three (1 large)	Mending seatless pants
Antacid	6 tablets	For indigestion or heartburn, may be Bucladin, Ulcetral, Rolaids	Salt tablets	24	To prevent exhaustion and cramps due to heavy perspiring
Antihistamine	6 tablets	1 every four hours for insect bites, colds or hives; may be Contac, Coryban D, etc.	Steri-pad gauze flats*	Six 4" × 4"	For large abrasions
			Tape, nonwaterproof*	2" roll	For sprains, securing dressings, etc.
Bandaids*	12—1 in.	For minor cuts	Triangular Bandage	One	For supporting arm and protecting dressing from contamination.
Butterfly Bandaids* (or know how to make them)	6 various sizes	For closing lacerations	First Aid and Rescue instructions	One	To ensure treatment is complete and correct. For splinting suspected forearm, wrist or ankle fractures
Large Compress Bandage	1 Kotex	For large bleeding wounds it is absolutely essential that clean absorbent dressings be applied completely over the wound with sufficient pressure to stop bleeding			
			Thermometer (Oral/Rectal Combination)	One	For determining temperature of victim or water when treating frostbite.
Molefoam*	1/2 pkg.	For padding blisters	Tweezers	One pair	For removing splinters
Needle	One med. size	To remove splinters, puncturing blisters, etc.	Prescription Medicines		For pain, sleep, insect bites, etc. To be used only by the person for which it was prescribed. If carried, each should be stored in its original container, clearly labelled as to dosage, purchase date, type of drug
Tincture of Benzoin	1 oz. bottle	To hold tape in place and protect the skin			
Antibacterial soap or Tincture of Zepherin	1 oz. bottle (plastic)	Mild antiseptic for abrasions, cuts			
Razor blade or small scissors		For cutting tape, molefoam, hair, loose bandage ends, etc.			

Those marked with an asterisk are the minimum requirements for a basic kit.

PART IV
RESOURCES

CHAPTER 17

WHERE TO BACKPACK

In spite of fears that North America is going to become a single urban sprawl laced with interstate highways, many millions of unpaved and unplotted acres remain for your enjoyment. Virtually every state and province has from thousands to millions of acres in public lands, from National Forests to National Parks to Bureau of Land Management acreage.

The federal government, with the cooperation of state and local governments, has established thousands of miles of trail systems throughout the continent, from the Lewis and Clark Trail that runs from St. Louis to Astoria, Oregon, along a system of rivers, to the Appalachian and Pacific Crest Trails. The latter two are marked and maintained while the Lewis and Clark is at this writing simply a route that is marked.

Every National Forest in America—and there are hundreds of them—has trail systems that are shown on the beautiful maps you can purchase at ranger stations or from the forest headquarters. These are usually preferable to National Parks because National Forests usually aren't so crowded. The scenery may be less spectacular, but solitude is easier to find.

Many large timber companies permit backpacking, as well as hunting and fishing in season, on their large holdings. Some, such as Weyerhaeuser Co., have sets of maps for sportsmen available at district offices.

A check with your local bookstore

will usually yield at least one hiking guide for your region, and many sporting goods stores stock books and maps for sportsmen that show trails, logging roads, and old mining trails. You can also join local hiking clubs or become involved with local scouting organizations or YMCAs and YWCAs.

Other good sources of information are outdoor outfitters, many of whom publish pamphlets or booklets with suggestions on outings.

If you are new to this form of recreation, word of mouth is also important, especially when hiking guidebooks don't exist or are sketchy in areas that interest you. Usually, however, the trails will be on public lands and someone on the land management staff will be familiar with the routes that interest you.

The major clubs that promote backpacking are listed below. Many have local chapters scattered across the continent, while others are committed to a particular area.

Adirondack Mountain Club, Gabriels, NY 12939.

American Hiking Society, 1255 Portland Place, Boulder, CO 80302.

Appalachian Mountain Club, 5 Joy Street, Boston, MA 02108.

Boy Scouts of America, PO Box 61030, Dallas/Ft. Worth, TX 75261.

National Audubon Society, 950 Third Ave., New York, NY 10022.

National Campers & Hikers Association, 7127 Transit Road, Buffalo, NY 14221.

National Hiking & Ski Touring Association, Box 7421, Colorado Springs, CO 80933.

National Wildlife Federation, 1412 16th St., NW, Washington, DC 20036.

Sierra Club, 530 Bush Street, San Francisco, CA 94108.

The Wilderness Society, 1901 Pennsylvania Ave., NW, Washington, DC 20006.

In addition to the Forest Service and National Park maps available at local offices, ranger stations and Government Bookstores, you should also own sets of topographical maps of the areas you'll backpack in. These are the most accurate maps available and are calibrated for the compass declination factor. Many backpackers buy two of each; one to keep because they're so attractive and to plan future trips, and the second to cut into small sections and keep in their pocket while on trips. Although each map can be folded and carried in a waterproof plastic cover, this severely limits their life span.

Many outdoor outfitters stock maps for their region; but if they are not available locally, you can obtain an index and ordering instructions by writing the addresses below:

East of the Mississippi: U.S. Geological Survey, Map Distribution Center, 1200 Eads Street, Arlington, VA 22202.

West of the Mississippi: U.S. Geological Survey, Map Distribution Center, Federal Center, Building 41, Denver, CO 80225.

Canada: Canadian Map Office, Department of Energy, Mines and Resources, 614 Booth Street, Ottawa, Ontario K1A OE9.

Several hiking and conservation organizations and federal land management associations can also offer valuable written materials and guides to hiking areas.

American Hiking Society
18600 S.W. 157 Avenue
Miami, Florida 33187

Appalachian Trail Conference
P.O. Box 236
Harpers Ferry, West Virginia 25425

Federation of Western Outdoor Clubs
4534 1/2 University Way N.E.
Seattle, Washington 98105

New England Trail Conference
P.O. Box 145
Weston, Vermont 05161

Sierra Club
530 Bush Street
San Francisco, California 94108

Wilderness Society
1901 Pennsylvania Avenue N.W.
Washington, D.C. 20006

United States Forest Service
Department of Agriculture
Washington, D.C. 20250

National Park Service
Department of the Interior
Washington, D.C. 20240

Bureau of Land Management
Department of the Interior
Interior Building
Washington, D.C. 20240

Fish and Wildlife Service
Department of the Interior
Interior Building
Washington, D.C. 20240

CHAPTER 18

FURTHER READING

Angier, Bradford. **Field Guide to Edible Wild Plants**. Harrisburg, Pennsylvania: Stackpole, 1976.

The Audubon Society Field Guide Series. New York: Alfred A. Knopf, 1979-81.

Barker, Harriett. **Supermarket Backpacker**. Chicago: Contemporary Books, 1977.

Bradford, Angier. **How To Stay Alive in the Woods**. New York: Collier, 1976.

Doan, Marlyn. **Starting Small in the Wilderness**. San Francisco: Sierra Club, 1979.

Ferber, Peggy, ed. **Mountaineering: The Freedom of the Hills**. Seattle: The Mountaineers, 1974.

Fletcher, Colin. **The Man Who Walked Through Time**. New York: Alfred A. Knopf, 1968.

———. **The New Complete Walker**. New York: Alfred A. Knopf, 1974.

Ganci, Dave. **Hiking the Desert**. Chicago: Contemporary Books, 1979.

Gibbon, Euell. **Stalking the Blue-Eyed Scallop**. New York: David McKay, 1962.

———. **Stalking the Wild Asparagus**. New York: David McKay, 1962.

Hare, James, ed. **From Katahdin to Springer Mountain**. Emmaus, Pennsylvania: Rodale Press, 1977.

Hillcourt, William. **The Official Boy Scout Handbook**. New Brunswick, New Jersey: Boy Scouts of America, 1979.

Kemsley, William. **Backpacking Equipment Buyer's Guide**. New York: Collier, 1978.

———. **The Whole Hiker's Handbook**. New York: William Morrow, 1979.

Kjellstrom, Bjorn. **Be Expert with Map and Compass**. New York: Charles Scribner's Sons, 1976.

Lathrop, Theodore G., M.D. **Hypothermia: Killer of the Unprepared**. Portland, Oregon: The Mazamas, 1972.

Manning, Harvey. **Backpacking: One Step at a Time**. New York: Vintage, 1980.

Olsen, Larry Dean. **Outdoor Survival Skills**. Provo, Utah: Brigham Young University Press, 1973.

Rugge, John, and James West Davidson. **The Complete Wilderness Paddler**. New York: Alfred A. Knopf, 1977.

Rustrum, Calvin. **The Wilderness Routefinder**. New York: Collier, 1967.

Van Lear, Denise, ed. **The Best About Backpacking**. San Francisco: The Sierra Club, 1974.

INDEX